Contents

Introduction

Practice is a lot like exercise. You know you have to do it, but sometimes it can feel like a chore. However, finding the right exercises for you – the ones you actually enjoy – puts you on the road to lifelong fitness. This book is designed to increase and enhance your "bass fitness" for life!

Each exercise is written to sound like a real bassline, solo, fill or chord progression. They work on specific techniques alongside aspects of music like harmony, rhythm, groove, fretboard knowledge, ear training and genres stylistics. By the time you have completed this book, you will be able to navigate the fretboard better, will have a stronger ear, and know how to use arpeggios and scales to make music. As well, of course, as having better technique…

Technique is a means to an end. It is an essential tool required to express yourself freely. Sloppy technique leads to frustration and minimises what it is possible for you to play. A dedicated approach to improving all aspects of your technique will undoubtedly lead to you becoming a better bass player. Add in all the other musical skills and you have a recipe for complete musicianship.

Where possible, I have included examples of basslines that use the exercise presented, or ways that you can use it yourself. I have found that I am (along with many students over the years) much more likely to work on exercises designed to push my technical ability if they sound like music. There is a time and a place for repetitive, mechanical exercises, but you won't find them in this book. (Well, OK, maybe a couple!)

Chapter One begins with various exercises based around the chords of a harmonised major scale. This is the foundation of many styles of music and is the key to being able to groove musically. The remaining chapters explore exercises based around pop, blues/RnB, funk, rock and jazz. Chapter Seven will develop your ear training by using drones alongside the example to hear the musical effect of the exercise.

CREATIVE **BASS**
TECHNIQUE EXERCISES

70 Melodic Exercises To Develop Great Feel & Technique on Bass Guitar

DAN **HAWKINS**

FUNDAMENTAL**CHANGES**

Creative Bass Technique Exercises

70 Melodic Exercises to Develop Great Feel & Technique on Bass Guitar

ISBN: 978-1-78933-056-4

Published by **www.fundamental-changes.com**

Copyright © 2019 Dan Hawkins

Edited by Tim Pettingale

www.fundamental-changes.com

Twitter: @guitar_joseph

Over 10,000 fans on Facebook: **FundamentalChangesInGuitar**

Instagram: **FundamentalChanges**

For over 350 Free Guitar Lessons with Videos Check Out

www.fundamental-changes.com

Get the Audio

The audio files for this book are available to download for free from **www.fundamental-changes.com.** The link is in the top right-hand corner. Just select this book title from the drop-down menu and follow the instructions to get the audio.

We recommend that you download the files directly to your computer, not to your tablet, and extract them there before adding them to your media library. You can then put them on your tablet, iPod or burn them to CD. On the download page there is a help PDF and we also provide technical support via the contact form.

For over 350 Free Guitar Lessons with Videos Check out:

www.fundamental-changes.com

Twitter: **@guitar_joseph**

Over 10,000 fans on Facebook: **FundamentalChangesInGuitar**

Instagram: **FundamentalChanges**

The Fundamentals

Being able to play bass well means having a range of internalised techniques under your fingers that you can call on automatically. Some of those techniques are flashy, such as slapping and tapping, but many are more mundane (but crucial), such as string dampening. This book works on the fundamental techniques that you need in order to play with fantastic feel and great tone:

• Fingerstyle

• Left and right hand coordination, speed, strength and accuracy

• Hammer-ons

• Pull-offs

• Slides

• Rakes

• Position shifts

• Ghost notes

• Muting/dampening

There are also some slap, tap and plectrum exercises. If you hear an example that you think would work played with a plectrum or slapped, but isn't notated accordingly, I encourage you to experiment.

How To Use These Exercises

There are only two rules when it comes to technique:

1) Ensure your mechanics (the coordination between hands and mind) are as close to perfect as you can get, so you can execute the technique effortlessly with a nice clean sound.

2) Do the above with no pain or strain. This will help you avoid any problems in the future.

Hold the bass so that the neck is immediately accessible to your fretting hand and ensure your wrist and hand are as straight as possible. Curling your fingers and playing on the fingertips allows you to fret the notes while keeping a straight and relaxed wrist (there will be a tiny bit of bend, but there shouldn't be too much).

When sitting, I like to angle the neck at roughly forty-five degrees to the back of my chair and have the head facing towards the ceiling a tiny bit. I ensure the body of the bass is in contact with three points – my leg, my chest and my forearm (somewhere near the elbow). This ensures that I don't hold the neck with my fretting hand. Grabbing hold of the neck is a bad habit that restricts what your fretting hand can do. We need that hand free to do lots of amazing bass playing!

Some people like to hold the instrument in a classical guitar like posture. Experiment with where the bass sits until you are relaxed and comfortable. Breath normally and relax the muscles in your body when you play. Often, the first thing to happen when you are confronted with something difficult is to tense up and hold your breath. Relaxing into your playing makes you groove better and avoids strain and tension in the fingers and wrists. This is the beginning of great technique, so read the last two paragraphs again and keep this advice in mind whenever you practise.

If you feel any pain whatsoever, stop immediately. Start again the next day, but if the pain persists see your doctor. The bass is a large instrument that requires good technique. You do not need to have long fingers to play bass – just good technique!

I have included fretting hand fingerings throughout and, where appropriate, some for the plucking hand. Everyone has different sized fingers and a unique hand stretch, so if you find a way to play an exercise that works better for you then I encourage you to explore that.

There are audio examples for every exercise so give those a listen, especially if you come across any notation or rhythms that look a little complex. There are a few nasty-looking examples but don't worry, they look far more difficult than they actually are!

To master some of these exercises you may have to take a look at the way you practice. The way to approach anything you find difficult is to calmly break down the passage and focus on the tricky parts. Analyse what both hands are doing, how you are holding the bass, your posture, and then slowly identify what needs to improve. You build great technique by deliberately practising correct movements over and over again. These are the fundamentals that allow you to play music without worrying about technique. That is your ultimate goal.

Finally, strive for precision, accuracy, groove and great feel in everything you play. As you go through the exercises, look for different patterns or ways to approach the exercises. Make them your own. If you hear something that may work in a solo or a song then use it. Finding your own voice as a bass player is one of the most important goals you can have, so experiment and see what works for you.

With a consistent practice routine and the right exercises, you can achieve the technique you have always wanted.

Harmonised Scale Exercises

Along with rhythm and melody, harmony is one of the foundations that music is built on. A clear understanding of how to use the notes found within a scale will transform the way you play.

• When you harmonise (build a chord from every note of) a major scale, you create seven chords.

• Every major scale has a relative minor scale which contains the same seven chords starting from a different place.

Those two short sentences hint at how a huge amount of music is made. Most songs and tunes use the chords constructed from either the major or relative minor scale. The exercises in this chapter all explore the scales and arpeggios that come from these chords and focus on different ways of playing a harmonised scale. These ideas can be used in basslines, solos, fills and in your song writing.

Don't worry if the theory eludes you for now, the point is to play exercises that will unlock the fretboard as well as sharpen your ear and build your technique.

~

Example 1a is an arpeggio-based idea that walks through the *7th arpeggios* formed on each note of the major scale.

This example is a fantastic workout for both the fretting and plucking hands, as well as providing plenty of practice playing along the length of the fretboard.

As is always the case, there is more than one way to play this exercise. However, focus on the fingering patterns provided as they teach you a comfortable way of navigating these arpeggios. If you do find different patterns, go ahead and work on those too. The best way is always the most efficient one that allows you to play a line easily with no straining in the wrists or fingers.

You will notice there are quite a few shifts in this exercise. For example, when moving from Cmaj7 to Dm7 your first finger needs to travel from the 2nd fret of the D string (E) to the 5th fret of the A string (D). That's a jump of four frets and takes some getting used to. Focus on nailing this jump so that you don't hear any gaps between the notes and ensure the notes flow by smoothly and accurately.

Look at the chord symbols above the notes and memorise them. These are the chords (and arpeggios for you as a bass player) that are formed from a harmonised major scale.

Example 1a

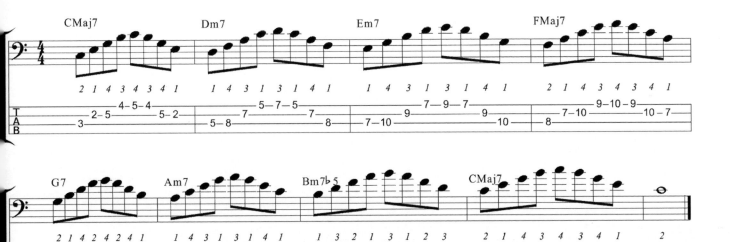

Bass players don't usually play chords, but they can sound great and be used in a number of situations. Exercise 1b introduces classical guitar right-hand fingering notation, where you pluck the notes with your thumb (p), index (i) and middle (m) fingers. Each digit has its own string which it sticks to.

When you play chords, curl your fretting hand fingers and play right on the fingertips to avoid choking any strings. Normally when you pluck a note, your finger should come to rest on the string below. This is called a *rest stroke*. However, when playing chords in the following example, play *free stroke*. This is where you pluck away from the body of the bass and allow the strings to ring out, undampened.

Depending on your reach, you may want to play the D minor and E minor chords in bars two and three with the left-hand fingering 3 1 4 instead of the written 2 1 3. If you feel any strain or pain in your fretting hand, then stop. Build up the stretch slowly on this one.

Notice that the sequence of chords is the same as in Example 1a. This is the chord sequence created from a harmonised C Major scale and is worth memorising because the sequence of chord types (Major, Minor, Minor, Major, Major, Minor 7b5) is the same in any major key.

Here are three ways to create music from Example 1b.

• Repeat the example but alter the rhythm and the order of notes within the chord. For example, in the first bar instead of playing C, E, G, play E, C, G.

• Many songs are built from these chords, so try playing them in different orders to find *progressions* that you like, for example C major, F major, A minor, G major. Then experiment by altering the plucking patterns and the rhythms. You will start to hear some music forming!

• Use rest strokes instead of free strokes.

Example 1b

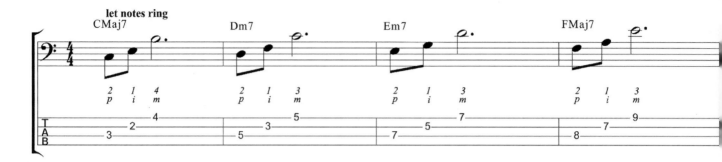

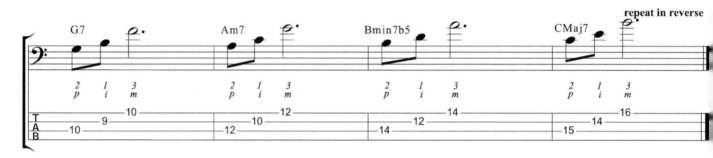

So far in this chapter we have played both arpeggios and chords. Along with scales, these are what basslines are made from.

Example 1c moves to the key of G Major (but notice how the order of chord *types* is exactly the same as in C Major).

This exercise ascends the *mode* starting on each degree of the G Major scale and descends the *pentatonic scale* that fits over that chord. The pentatonic scale is either major or minor depending on whether the mode is major or minor.

There is an incredible amount of useable information in this one exercise alone. Memorise which modes and pentatonic scales fit over each chord.

Use consistent, alternating index and middle fingers throughout, after executing the pull off found at the beginning of each descending pentatonic scale.

Start slowly, setting your metronome at 80 bpm (beats per minute) or below, then gradually build some speed

Example 1c

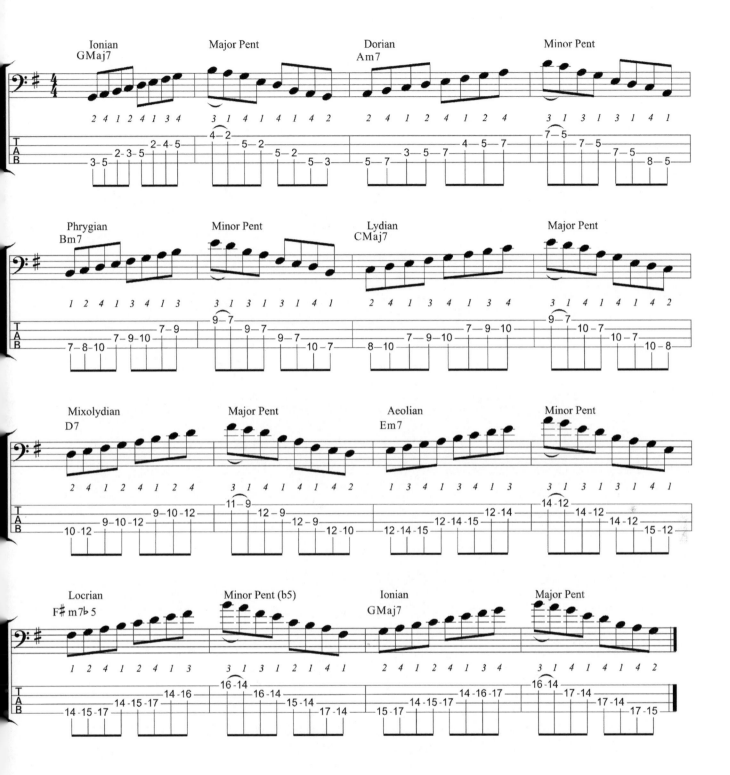

The next exercise is good for developing string crossing in your plucking hand and for ear training.

Each arpeggio in this example uses a set pattern of intervals from the chord: Root, 5th, Octave, 3rd and 11th. Map each interval visually on the fretboard relative to the root note. These notes are always found in basslines and fills and will help you to unlock the fretboard. Get used to the sounds that these patterns create and memorise the name of the interval.

Once you are comfortable with the exercise, play the arpeggios in different orders to create chord sequences. For example, Fmaj7, Am7, Dm7, Bbmaj7.

While this can sound like a boring exercise, you can make it sound more like a bassline or solo by altering the rhythms and phrases you play. Remember that major and minor pentatonic scales fit over these chords too, so try adding in some of those sounds.

Example 1d

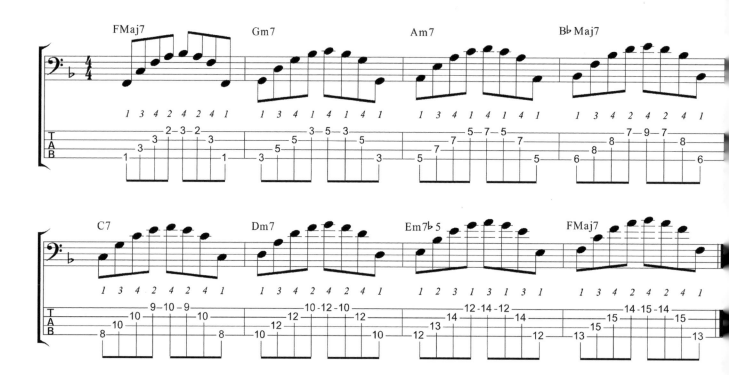

By playing an arpeggio in the order Root, 5th, 3rd, then descending the notes of the scale, we create a Bach-like sound. The Bach Cello Suites are a great favourite of bass players and provide a fun technical challenge.

Example 1e offers some challenging fretting hand fingering, so pay attention and follow the patterns closely. The exercise works its way high up the fretboard, so anticipate where your fingers need to be before they play the notes. This is the key to playing smoothly and accurately.

Notice how you lead with your second finger in every bar except three and seven where it is your first finger. Be ready for those bars as an extra position shift is required there.

Fret with care and mute the strings with your plucking hand so that no extra noise is heard. Do this by anchoring your plucking hand thumb on the string below the one you're playing. So, for example, rest on the low E string when playing notes on the A string. When playing the E string you can anchor on a pickup.

Learn to move naturally and automatically between these muting positions. It takes a bit of getting used to, but it's an essential technique for clean and accurate playing. Record yourself playing all kinds of different lines and exercises and listen back to identify and kill any offending noise that's easy to miss in the moment. I remember hearing all kinds of horrific things going on the first time I tried this!

Example 1e

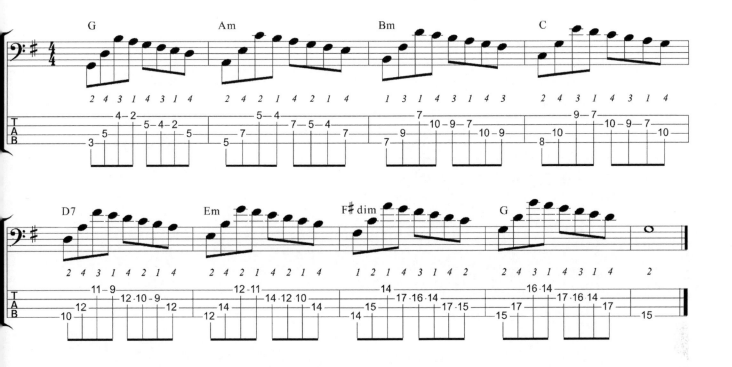

The next example is in the key of F Major and is based on playing a 7th chord followed by a cool pentatonic line.

Learning this relationship between chords and pentatonic scales allows you to play exciting ideas over these chords when you write basslines and improvise.

Due to the wider fret gaps in the first few frets of the bass, you might find it easier to use your fourth finger in the first bar as indicated. However, feel free to replace that with the third finger if you prefer.

Pay attention to the hammer-ons and time them so that the 1/8th notes remain steady throughout. Bar seven (Em7b5) requires a slightly odd hand position due to the b5 (flat fifth) present in the chord. Barre your first finger across the fretboard so that the tip of the finger frets the note as usual, while the bottom of the finger near the knuckle frets the 12th fret on the G string.

Example 1f

Example 1g works on a sweet-sounding fingerstyle line using an E *pedal* note. A pedal note is a bass note that stays the same while the chords or melody changes on top.

The chord progression is I IV iii ii in the key of E Major (E major, A major, G#m, F#m), and the chord shapes should be familiar from Example 1b. The sound of chords moving around over a pedal note is a common one in music and good to get your ear used to.

Sound the pedal note by plucking the open E string with your thumb. The root of each chord is played with the picking hand thumb, the 3rd with the index, and the 7th with the middle finger. Memorise the shapes and the intervals so you can improvise with them whenever you see the relevant chord symbol.

Example 1g

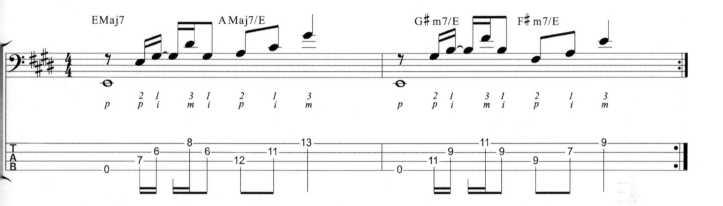

The next two exercises are monsters related to the beast in Example 1b! In order to fit all the arpeggios onto the fretboard, this one is in the key of F# Major. It looks a lot scarier than it actually is, but again, notice that it contains the same order of chords and patterns. However, this is a challenging exercise and I advise you to slowly learn two bars at a time. It's a tough one to execute at speed, so instead, aim to play this with no stumbles or mistakes. Use alternate plucking.

Descend one arpeggio beginning with a pull-off and ascend the next beginning with a hammer-on.

The arpeggio in each bar contains a two-string pattern that is moved up an octave. So in bar one, the final four notes are exactly the same as the first four notes, just one octave lower. Visualise each bar as one two-string pattern which you then move one octave.

There are two tricky shifts. The first is when you shift from one two-string pattern to the next. The second is the transition from one arpeggio to the next.

For example, in bar one the fourth finger of your fretting hand plays the first note (C# on the 6th fret of the G string) before playing the C# one octave lower (4th fret A string). To get this smooth, begin shifting your thumb as soon as you have finished playing the first note. Get the fourth finger as close as you can to the 4th fret of the A string *before* it is needed.

The whole exercise should be approached in this way: with the fretting hand fingers moving to the next note a split second before it is required.

Example 1h

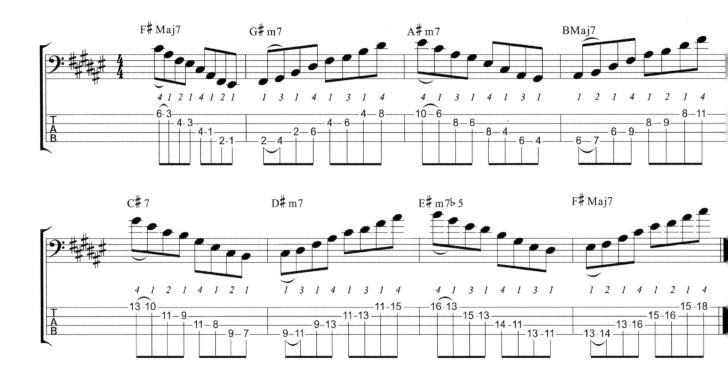

Example 1i is simply the same thing in reverse. Once you have both Example 1g and 1h down, combine them into one mega-exercise to improve your stamina.

Example 1i

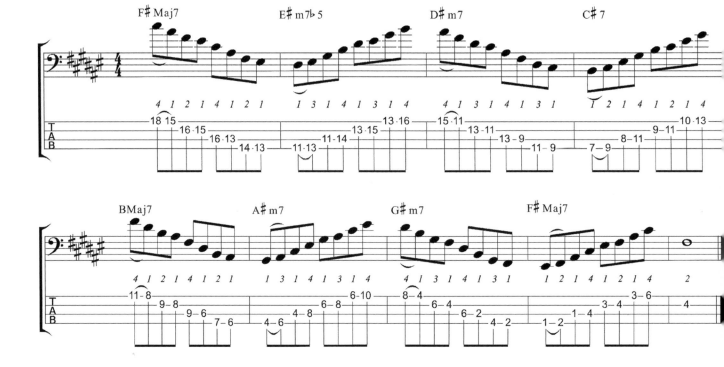

We finish this chapter with a real speed builder that will tax your coordination, fluency and accuracy. It needs to be learnt slowly because this exercise uses 1/16th note triplets (six notes every beat). Get this under your fingers slowly at around 40 bpm before speeding up, and listen to the audio to hear what it should sound like. Lots of impressive fast music involves playing 1/16th note triplets so they are well worth adding to your repertoire.

Every time you move to a new arpeggio you shift higher up the neck by leading with your fourth finger. This will feel like a leap of faith at first, but that's why you practise at slow tempos.

On the minor seventh arpeggios, wherever the second finger is indicated, you can use your third finger instead if you prefer. Try both ways and see which you like. Either way, those minor seventh shapes require a five fret stretch rather than the normal four, which is a good work out for the hands.

Ensure you are holding the bass correctly so that your fretting hand wrist is as straight as possible and the neck is readily accessible as described in the introduction.

Due to the stretches involved in this exercise it's possible you may feel some strain in the fretting hand wrist. Stop if this is the case. Take a rest or come back to it tomorrow. Do not push through the pain barrier as this is a ticket to tendonitis.

Example 1j

Pop

Although in pop music the main job of the bass player is to provide a solid foundation for the music and play with great feel, not all pop playing is simple. Some of the exercises in this chapter will take a while to master, but they will help to sharpen your timing. With all of these exercises, the emphasis is on playing melodic, interesting lines that groove.

Example 2a is an 1/8th note workout in D Major over a IV V vi (G major, A major, Bm) chord progression. This feel is common in pop, but not as easy to play as people think.

Set your metronome to 100bpm and sit with this groove until the fretting hand shifts are smooth and you can play the line with confidence. When you can play it comfortably, try increasing the tempo slowly up to 120bpm.

Concentrate on playing this exercise evenly with no rushing or slowing down, and follow the fingering pattern as indicated. Watch out for the first finger stretching out to the 5th fret in bar three.

Example 2a

Example 2b is another workout designed to help you play 1/8th notes confidently and in time. For this exercise I recommend using a plectrum. If you play mostly with fingers, using a plectrum can feel alien, but it can be extremely effective for this style of playing.

Use anchoring to keep your hand steady, so that your pick attack is even and consistent. There are many ways to anchor, but start by resting the top of your forearm (somewhere near the elbow) on the cutaway at the top of the bass body. Adjust the placement until your plectrum hovers around the strings. That alone will give you more control. I use down strokes for all the notes in this exercise, but feel free to try alternate picking if you prefer.

Your fretting hand will remain in one position, giving you the chance to strengthen your fourth finger. Set the metronome to around 120bpm for this exercise.

Pay attention to the muting between notes. Your plectrum hand will be busy and you need to ensure that your fretting hand doesn't accidentally pluck a string as a finger releases a note. Work on your fretting hand muting until you can play this cleanly and accurately, and listen to the audio example to hear how it sounds.

Example 2b

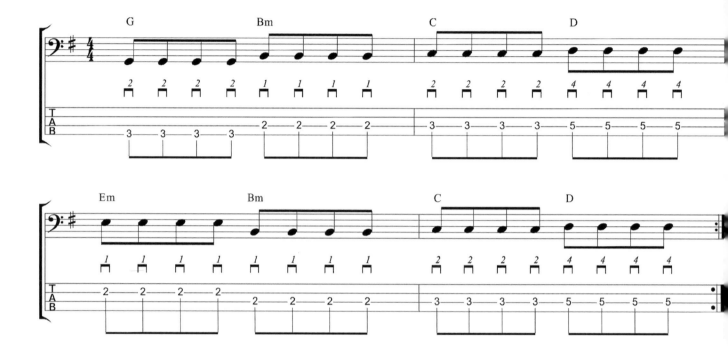

Playing octaves on bass spells DISCO! They're actually used in many styles and playing them accurately is the name of the game here. This exercise is played on a i VI III VII (Bm, G major, D major, A major) chord sequence in the key of B Minor.

Use your fourth finger throughout to play the higher octave note. It may feel weak at first, but this is a great exercise to strengthen it. You *can* use your third finger, but pay close attention to any signs of strain or fatigue in the fingers, hands or wrist.

In the plucking hand, start with your index, then play the octave with the middle finger. The whole exercise uses this pattern. Keep the notes even and steady and experiment with the note length. Keeping them all short and *staccato* will sound quite '70s but lengthening the notes will change the feel slightly.

Example 2c

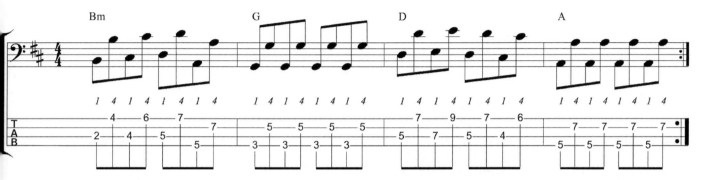

The next example cranks things up a notch. It is in the same key as the previous example, but this time played on a iv VII III VI (Em, A major, D major, G major) sequence. You can actually play both these examples together and they will fit.

The 1/16th notes and the staccato 1/8ths give the plucking hand much more of a workout, and the fretting hand requires a light touch to execute the staccato. Listen to *Dance Dance Dance* by Chic for a great example of this kind of rhythmic octaves bassline.

A specific plucking pattern may sometimes be required to make a line breathe and play it smoothly. Here, the rhythm on beat 1 is played by plucking the A string with your index finger, then immediately playing the following note with the same finger. This sets up the middle finger to play the next 1/16th note. As soon as the middle finger strikes the G string, get the index finger back to the E string in anticipation of the next note on the A string. This fingering pattern is essential when playing lines where there is a *string-skip* jump.

The short staccato notes are created by your fretting hand. As soon as the note is played, lift the finger off the note while maintaining light contact with the string. As soon as the finger is relaxed, the note stops and becomes short and detached. This is a tricky little technique to master, but absolutely essential for great bass playing.

Note length is so important in giving lines life, flair, groove and feel, so work on being able to control it. Once you have this exercise down try combining it with Example 2c.

Example 2d

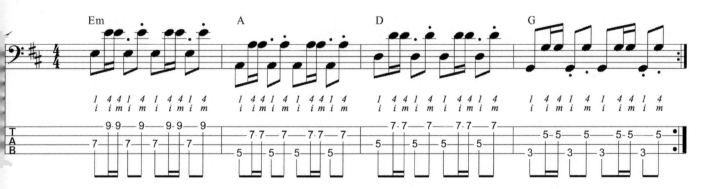

Inversions allow a smooth and musical connection between chords. An inversion occurs when you play a note of an arpeggio other that the root as the bass note of the chord (normally the first note in the bar). Inversions are notated using *slash* chords, for example, G/B means "a G chord with the note B in the bass". The chord has been "inverted" since a pitch other than the root is played as the lowest note in the chord.

If the chord sequence was G major to C major, you would play G to C. The smoother transition of B to C happens when the first chord is inverted (G/B to C Major).

Example 2e explores this idea while smoothly transitioning from the second to the fifth position on the fretboard. Pino Palladino used this to great effect on *New York Minute* by Don Henley. There are also some hammer-ons and pull-offs in bar two to give your fretting hand a good workout.

Ensure that you closely follow the fingering patterns that guide your fretting hand across the fretboard via a series of hand shifts. Practise each shift slowly aiming for no stops or sudden movements of the fretting hand. In the final bar, use the thumb and the first finger of your picking hand to play the *double stop*. A double stop is when you play two notes at the same time and is a fantastic device to use in your bass playing to add a bit of harmony. They work great on an ending.

Example 2e

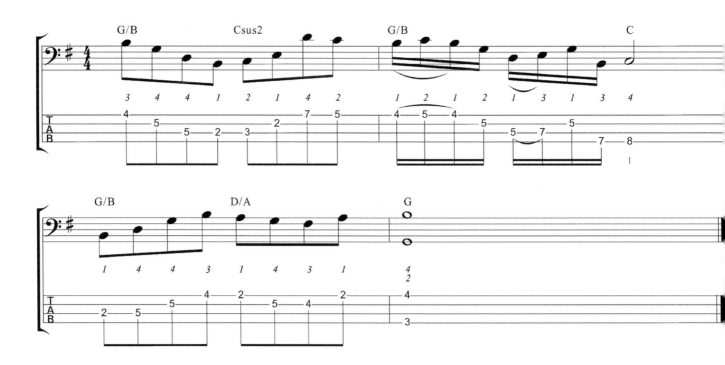

Example 2f is a V vi IV V (G major, A minor, F major, G major) progression in C Major based around a pretty-sounding pattern using the 9th interval of the chord. Used like this, the intervals sound great in ballads – one famous example being the guitar line in the intro of *Every Breath You Take* by The Police.

The first two notes in each bar are played using the first finger of the fretting hand, allowing easy access to the 9th interval, which is played with the third finger. Use that same finger to slide to the 3rd (10th). Apply some gentle vibrato and play with as much feeling as you can!

The target speed for this exercise is 100bpm but your fretting hand will have to shift quickly to make this exercise sound smooth and musical, so nail those shifts at a slower tempo.

Each bar calls for your hand to move a span of five or six frets. That's quite a distance, so ignore your metronome until you have the line under your fingers.

A good habit is to play anything new or difficult slowly until you are comfortable with it before playing it up to speed, concentrating on the time and feel. This is where you can introduce your metronome, drum beat or – even better – a real drummer.

Example 2f

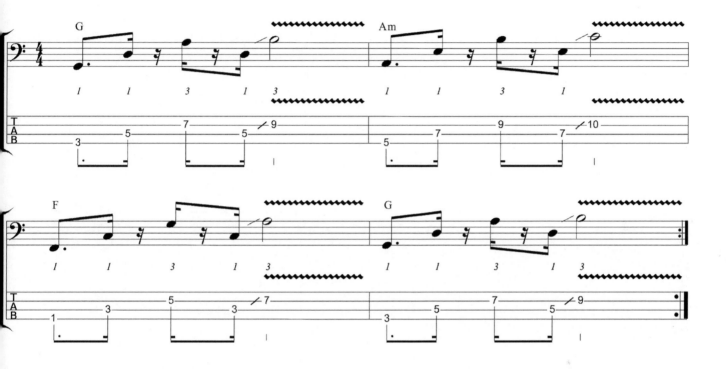

Example 2g develops your hammer-ons, pull-offs, slides and position shifts using a couple of useful shapes while ascending the first four chords of C Major (C major, D minor, E minor, F major).

Pay close attention to the notes played under each chord. You will notice that the same two shapes are played for each minor and major chord. These are both common sounds heard in many different styles of music.

The slides in this exercise come from below. Fret the note two frets below your target, pick it and then slide into the target note.

Example 2g

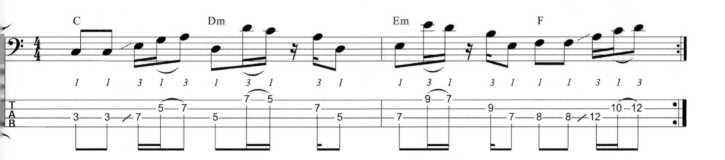

While all the examples in this chapter have used a *straight feel*, Example 2h introduces a funky 1/16th note *swing* feel. Listen to the audio example to hear exactly how this should be played.

When you slide up to the D note on the G string (7th fret), use your fretting hand thumb as a pivot on the back of the neck when you slide with your fourth finger. Don't shift the thumb across the back of the neck. Instead, rotate your wrist keeping the thumb tip in the same position and use it as a pivot. This makes it easier to return to the 3rd fret without having to shift again.

Great technique is about developing economy of motion and removing unnecessary effort. Think of Roger Federer hitting a backhand winner down the line at Wimbledon: effortless!

You may recognise the sound of the Dorian mode in the final bar and it sounds similar to the bassline in *Good Times* by Chic. Associating a shape, pattern or scale with a well-known melody or bassline is a brilliant way to train your ear. Always look to build your library of useful connections with ideas like this one.

Example 2h

Example 2i packs in quite a few techniques: Double-stops, position shifts and a pentatonic line using hammer-ons.

The move from the first two notes in each bar to the double-stops requires good dexterity in the fretting hand. Isolate that part and slowly repeat it. Twist your wrist a little to get the first finger from the E string all the way to the G string. Use the index and middle fingers of your fretting hand to pluck the double-stops.

The offbeat 1/16th notes in beat 2 are quite tricky to execute in time, so concentrate on nailing those. Set your metronome to 80bpm and play the first of those 1/16ths immediately after beat 2.

Tap your foot on the beats to get used to where you need to place a note in relation to your foot. This is also good practice for reading rhythms. Every note must be played somewhere in a bar and if you are confident about where the beats are, and can subdivide them well, you will play with confidence and authority.

Listen to Tony Levin's bassline on *Don't Give Up* by Peter Gabriel to hear a fantastic example of double-stops in a pop setting.

Example 2i

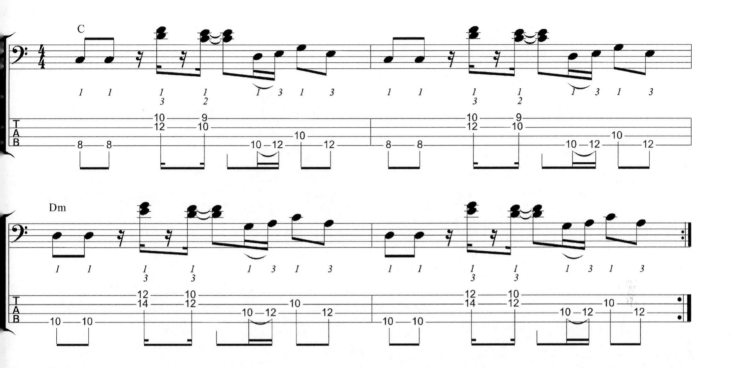

One of the brilliant things about the bass guitar is that you can play so many different styles and techniques. Most bass playing calls for solid, tasteful, groovy playing that provides a foundation for the band. Example 1g, however, is more of a melody line that could easily be played by a guitar or keyboard.

This line develops your compositional and improvisational skills. You can use variations of this exercise in your solos and fills too, since minor chords occur so often in many styles of music.

The exercise uses the i iv and v chords (G minor, C minor, D minor) in the key of G Minor and contains a minor pentatonic scale played across all four strings on the neck. The pattern over each chord is identical. Hammer your third finger onto the higher note, then immediately play the same fret one string lower with the same finger. In order to do this, *roll* your third finger from the higher string to the lower one. This way of fingering keeps the fourth finger ready and prepared for the note it is about to play. Study the TAB and fingering marks and you'll see what I mean.

This kind of attention to technical detail is how you gain accuracy, speed and fluency in your playing. Start slowly and build from there. Take your time exploring the idea and allow your brain time to understand what your hands and fingers should be doing. This approach builds muscle memory but requires patience and consistency.

Example 2j

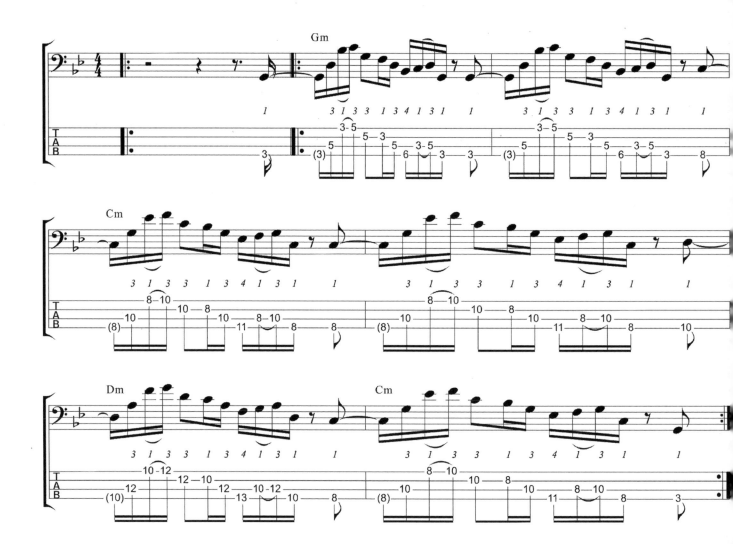

Blues/RnB

Studying different styles, genres and players from history gives you an important perspective from which to learn. Blues is the precursor of most modern music, from jazz to rock n roll, RnB to pop. Even when playing pop, rock and funk you will recognise some of the basslines that the first blues players pioneered. This realisation gives a clear picture of how all the different musical styles and genres are related. Not only is this a great source of inspiration to keep learning new music, it also makes playing easier, as you can borrow ideas from basslines you already know.

The examples in this chapter showcase some of the main features of blues and RnB bass playing.

Example 3a is a simple blues pattern based around a I IV V IV (G major, C major, D major, C major) chord progression in G Major. This is one of the essential chord sequences in blues and is found in many styles of pop and rock.

Start with your second finger on the 3rd fret of the E string (G). Follow the finger pattern for the rest of the notes in the bar, making sure you stretch your fourth finger to the D on the 5th fret of the A string. This exact pattern is repeated on the root note of each chord. Keep all the notes connected smoothly and work on the coordination between your fretting and picking hands.

This simple pattern will work over any major chord symbol, so memorise it and play it in different keys. The more you learn lines and licks that fit over chords, the more you can call on them when you play.

When you have this exercise mastered, try changing the order of the notes. This will give you some more patterns to work on.

Example 3a

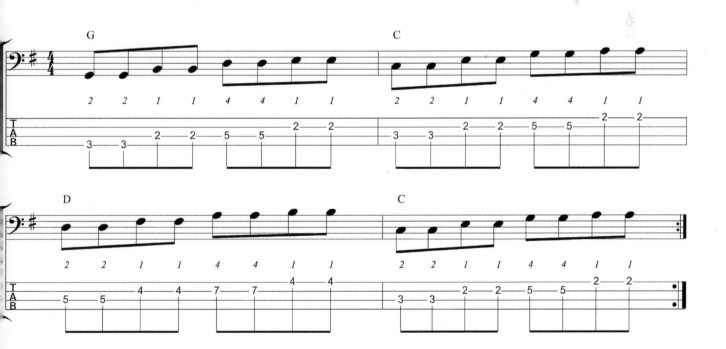

Example 3b introduces the *dominant seventh* chords of G7 and C7. The dominant 7 chord *quality* takes you deep into blues territory. A seventh chord consists of the intervals Root, 3rd, 5th and b7. It is the b7 that creates the bluesy sound of the chord.

The notes of the chord G7 are G, B, D and F. Begin by sliding to the b7 (F on the 8th fret, A string) with your little finger before playing the 6th interval with your third finger, then the 5th of the chord with your first finger. Sliding with your fourth finger can be tricky, so go carefully there. Shift quickly back to the third fret to finish.

I highly recommend that you learn the intervals then map out their location on the fretboard. As you play this example, ensure you know which interval you are playing at any time, as this will teach you to play by ear confidently.

Example 3b

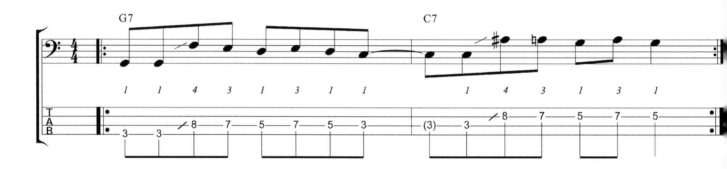

It's amazing how so many great blues and RnB basslines have been created using the same few intervals. Example 3c uses the 5th, major 6th and b7 again, but this time in a different pattern. Instead of ascending one string as we did in Example 3b, we now move from the A to the E string.

Rather than sliding up the fretboard to access the b7, we can now play it with the other notes in one hand position. Pay attention to the hammer-on from the first to the third finger.

Visually anchor where these intervals are, while getting used to their sounds. When you have this exercise down, alter the order of the third, fourth and fifth notes in each bar to create a new bassline.

Example 3c

One of the most important sounds of the blues is created by the *blues note* (b5) interval. It simply *is* the sound of the blues!

Another essential device is the use of the b3 to 3rd interval as a passing note.

Example 3d uses both these tricks, starting off with a hammer-on from the b3 to the 3 using the first and second fingers. This is a common thing to play in blues and RnB and you should try and add this sound into your lines.

After the hammer-on, shift up one fret and slide from the 6th to the 5th fret with your third finger. The note on the 6th fret is the blues note and it sounds great as a passing note. It sounds kind of "wrong" if you stay on that blues note too long, but it adds just the right amount of tension when used as a passing note.

This type of line is used in funk too and is a good example of how one style of music borrows innovations from other genres.

Example 3d

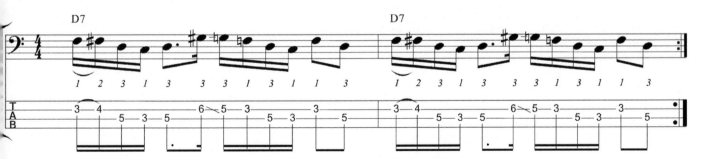

There are few more pleasing sounds in music than a great blues lick. Here's one that uses hammer-ons, pull-offs, slides and a quick hand shift with the blues scale. This is a pretty full-on workout that can be used in solo lines and fills. Set your metronome to around 80 bpm and go slow and steady for this.

Start by sliding from the 11th to the 10th fret with your third finger. You might recognise the blues note sound here. This is swiftly followed by the minor to major 3rd lick played with a hammer on. The second half of bar one is all alternate plucking with the index and middle fingers.

Bar two starts with two hammer-ons followed by a quick hand shift. This is probably the most difficult part of the exercise. Slide from fret 8 to fret 10 of the A string using the third finger and either pluck the string on the 8th fret (F) or slide without plucking. Try both ways as you will get a subtle difference in sound. The slide is performed with the third finger to put you in position to play the rest of the line without moving your fretting hand.

Once you have memorised this, move the exercise down the neck in semitones to practise playing in different keys. Any exercise you see in this book that contains patterns without open strings can also be shifted around. The uniform geometry of the bass allows you to play in different keys with relative ease.

Example 3e

Example 3f is an alternate fingering exercise. The 1/16th notes provide an opportunity to build speed and accuracy and to get the left and right hands coordinated.

Dominant seventh chords in blues are formed from the Mixolydian mode, which is the fifth mode of the major scale. Here, we run through the Mixolydian mode in a descending then ascending pattern.

As a bass player, knowing the right scale and arpeggio to use over any given chord is essential. The Mixolydian mode is the perfect scale to use on dominant seventh chords and is worth memorising so you can freely improvise over the dominant seventh chords in a blues progression. It gives you lots of options to use in the blues and RnB.

Closely follow the indicated fingering pattern which uses the one-finger-per-fret technique. Set your metronome to around 80 bpm and gradually build to the fastest speed at which you can play comfortably. Use this as a challenge to play as fast as you can (but always be in control, accurate and fluent!). Being able to execute 1/16th notes at a high tempo will set you up for any style of music and give you the strength, stamina and confidence you need to play the bass well.

Example 3f

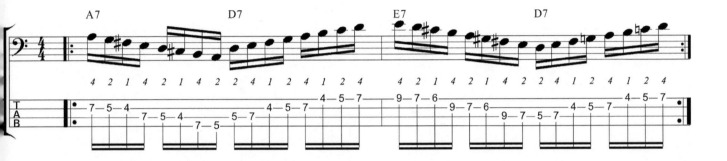

The *chromatic scale* contains all twelve semitones within an octave. The next example uses chromatics to connect notes from the chord to create a cool, familiar bassline. This syncopated exercise will test your groove and sense of rhythm, as well as your ability to shift smoothly on the fretboard.

In bar two, the second note is played with the fourth finger of your fretting hand, but the next note is just one fret lower and must be played with your first finger. This means that you have to pivot around your little finger (twisting your fretting hand wrist and moving your elbow into your body a little) to land on the 6th fret. This helps you transition smoothly from the fourth to the sixth position of the fretboard. The same thing happens in reverse between bars three and four.

This exercise helps you to navigate different areas of the fretboard and gives you greater range and more freedom to extend your basslines.

Example 3g

The next example proves that, in some situations, there is no such thing as a wrong note, and shows that adding chromatic notes where appropriate can add a real sophistication and hipness to your playing.

The exercise is based around a C7 arpeggio (C, E, G and Bb), but uses every other note from the chromatic scale to create a sense of forward momentum and tension.

Follow the suggested fingering pattern, but also try to find different ways to get from the 3rd to 10th fret. The way I suggest is pretty economical with the least number of position shifts and puts enough digits in the correct place to play the line comfortably. Any quick shift is going to be quite hard, so if you struggle, isolate that part and loop it to train your fingers.

Locate where the C7 notes (C, E, G and Bb) are in this exercise and analyse how the chromatic notes lead you to them. To work on your timing, set the metronome to 45 bpm and feel those clicks as beats "two" and "four" (this is the *backbeat* – when the snare drum hits on beats 2 and 4). This means that the tempo is actually 90 bpm, but you only hear half the number of clicks. Your internal clock needs to be bang on to fill in the gaps. Stay with it and loop the example until you feel yourself locking into the groove.

Example 3h

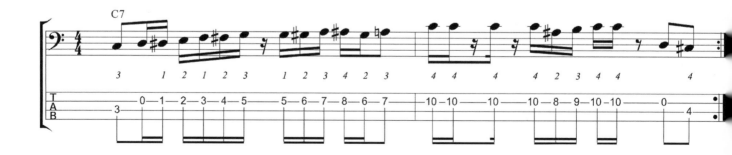

Blues basslines are often played with a shuffle feel in 12/8 and the next example explores this and adds some *syncopation* (off beat accents). Don't rush or pre-empt the syncopated notes in beats 3 and 4. Use your fourth finger to play anything on the 5th fret as the stretch is more comfortable that way. Although, if your third finger makes it more comfortable then feel free to use it.

The exception is in bar four, beat 3 where there is a difficult *bend and release*. Here, use your second finger to support your third finger for more control when you bend the note. Bend the 5th fret (C) up a semitone to C# then release back to C. The next note (Bb) is played on the third 1/8th note of that beat. Listen to the audio example to hear how it goes. Ensure you hit that bend and release confidently and play it in time.

Set your metronome to 100 bpm and count three 1/8th notes in every beat to feel the 12/8 groove. *Red House* by Jimi Hendrix is a good example of a slow 12/8 blues shuffle.

Example 3i

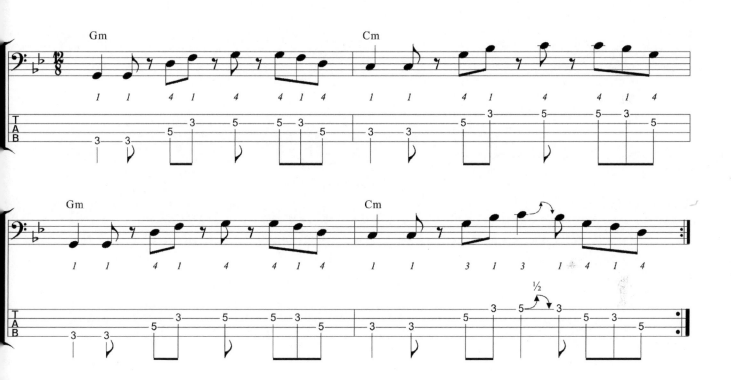

Example 3j contains many of the blues/RnB staples in one exercise. It is based around an E7 arpeggio and uses some chromatic notes around a simple E major chord in bar one. Bar two has a cool syncopated chromatic line leading to a run down the E Mixolydian scale in bar three. Bar four ends with an E7 arpeggio. Concentrate on linking each bar together smoothly and playing with great feel.

You can use all the ideas in this exercise in your basslines. Memorise the patterns and sounds. Visualise where the notes of the triad, arpeggio and mode are, and the sounds they create. This is as much an ear training exercise as it is a technical one.

The whole example takes place in sixth position (with your first finger located at the 6th fret) and the other fingers placed one per fret. There are a lot of creative basslines to be found in this one small area of the fretboard without moving your hand, so get exploring!

Example 3j:

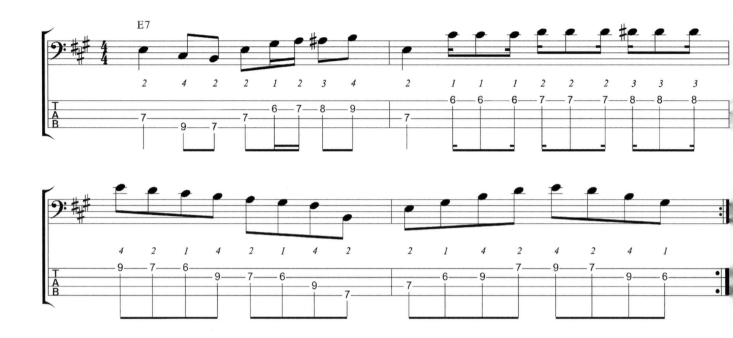

Funk

Funk basslines often feature syncopation and repetition. The "funk" comes from the way you play the notes and an unmistakable attitude is required in your touch. In this chapter the important *articulations* of funk bass playing are introduced. You can't mention funk without talking about *slap bass*, so you will find some cool exercises to work on that technique too. It is especially important in funk playing to be precise and play *in the pocket*, so using a metronome or drum machine is essential for all these examples. Despite many funk basslines requiring quite a lot of dexterity, there is often call for an aggressive, heavy plucking hand touch. Call on your best Bernard Edwards or Louis Johnson impression when you play these!

~

Francis Rocco Prestia III wrote the book on 1/16th note bass playing during his time with Tower of Power, and *Come On Come Over* on Jaco Pastorius' solo album is another great example of this style. It's incredibly satisfying to play, but hard to execute without rushing or slowing down. Practise Example 4a with a metronome to work on this skill. Aim to reach 120 bpm, but start much slower.

The fingering markings are important, especially at the end of the first bar where the final two notes are played with your fretting hand fourth finger. This gets your hand in the correct position to play the D on the 5th fret of the A string with your second finger.

Strictly alternate your plucking hand fingers between index and middle fingers, starting the line off with the index finger. When you're confident with that, switch and try starting with your middle finger. You will probably find that you prefer starting with one finger rather than the other. Go with that one.

When you practice this exercise slowed down, ensure that the fingers of both hands get to the next note or string just before you are due to play it, as this will build speed and accuracy. The mechanics between your hands need to be machine-like in their efficiency, so cut out as many unnecessary movements as you can. You may find yourself looking at your fretting hand more than your plucking hand, but check that both are doing exactly what they should be. Looking at only one hand can sometimes allow the other hand to get away with sloppy habits. Don't let that happen!

Example 4a

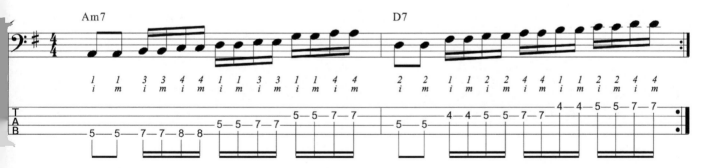

Ghost notes play a huge part in funk bass. This is where instead of applying pressure against the fretboard as you normally would, you touch the string without pressing down. This creates a dead, percussive sound which adds rhythm and groove, but not necessarily a pitch. However, this may sometimes create an accidental harmonic. To avoid this, don't press down directly over the fret. Instead, aim to be more "between" the two frets. Another common way to avoid a harmonic is to use more than one fingertip to play the ghost note. This ensures the string is muted completely and creates a satisfying thud.

Example 4b is inspired by Bernard Edwards of Chic who used these techniques to get feet tapping and songs grooving. Work through the notation, TAB and finger markings piece by piece. It helps to know that all you are playing is a simple G Minor pentatonic idea, so use this familiar pattern to help you get this down.

G Minor Pentatonic

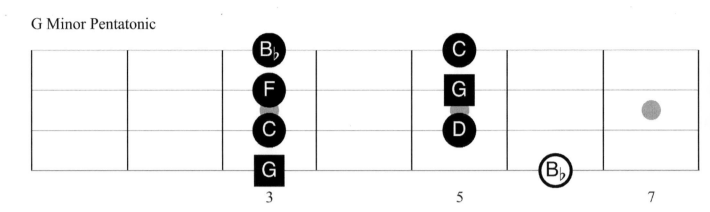

Example 4b

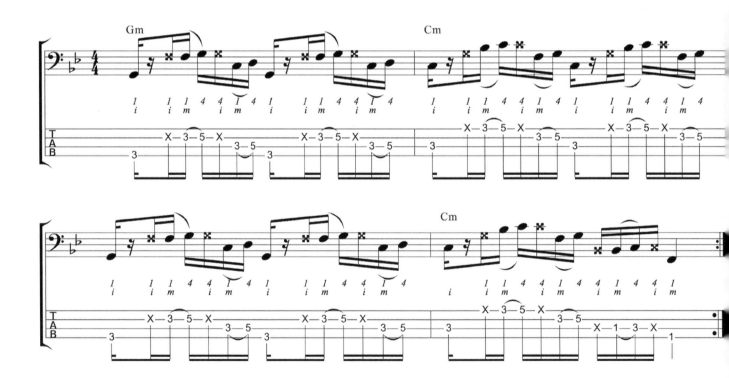

Example 4c again combines ghost notes and hammer-ons, but this time uses slap on a i III iv v sequence (F# minor, A major, B minor and C# minor) in the key of F# Minor. Follow the slap (S) and pop (P) markings closely here. The interplay between left and right hands when slapping is much like drumming and rhythms are created with fretting hand techniques just as much as the more obvious slaps and pops. Timing is critical here so get that metronome out.

The hammer-ons, pull-offs, ghost notes, slaps and pops are all in the same place when the chords move so once you get the first half of bar one down, the rest should flow from there.

Muting when slapping is incredibly important but often overlooked in favour of the more fun stuff going on. Your slapping hand will be too busy doing its thing to be muting, so your fretting hand will have to take up the slack here.

Let's take a closer look.

In bar one you can use your first finger to lightly hold the A, D and G strings while the E string is being fretted. The second and third fingers are not in use, so they too can mute.

In bar two the E string is not in use. Touch the tip of your first finger against the underside of the string to mute it. It's an awkward thing to get used to, but with practice will become second nature. The D and G strings are again held and muted by the first finger.

Use this exercise to build up your own string dampening technique. It's a relatively boring thing to have to do but it tightens up your playing and it will make you sound awesome. The difference between a decent player and a top level one are the small details like string dampening.

Example 4c

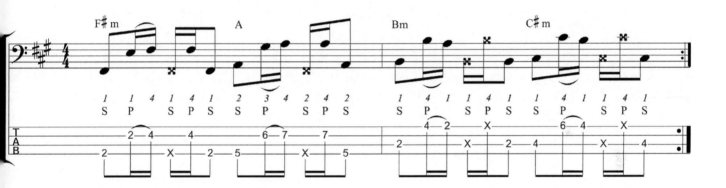

Funk lines often pack in many different articulations and the next exercise includes 1/16th note fingerstyle, hammer-ons, slides and hand shifts in one fluid line.

Your plucking hand is one of the tricky things to master in a line like this. With both slides and hammer-ons, the alternating plucking is interrupted. Keep the index and middle fingers alternating while ascending. On the way down, *rake* one finger from one string to the next if you find it easier.

In all honesty there are many, many plucking hand combinations for lines like this and there isn't a wrong way to do it as long as the line grooves. Experiment to see what works for you.

In bar one, slide to the note on the 11th fret from two frets below and keep your fretting hand thumb in the same place behind the neck as you do this. All notated slides in this example are to be played in this manner. The thumb acts as a pivot as you shoot the third finger up the neck and then immediately back again.

Bars three and four are identical. In the first slide, start on the 3rd fret with your third finger and shift the hand (sliding the fretting hand thumb across behind the neck) to land on the 5th fret with the same finger. Play the following slide as described in the previous paragraph. You can't approach these slides and shifts half-heartedly so go for it! Set the metronome to 90 bpm for this one and focus on accuracy. Make as many mistakes as you need to.

Example 4d

If you've ever heard Bobby Vega play then you know how amazingly funky a bass can sound when played with a pick. The key to playing funk styles with a plectrum is to keep a constant motion going with the plectrum hand. In Example 4e, this is shown by the plectrum markings and these will help you to be consistent in your placement of down and up strokes. Hit all the down beats with a down stroke and then subdivide each beat into 1/16th notes by playing down, up, down, up. Just keep that motion going and strike the strings on the notes you need to play.

Another feature of this exercise is the accents and ghost notes on beats 2 and 4. Feel the backbeat as that helps to brings out the funk. Follow the staccato notes closely as the contrast sounds cool.

Finally, there is a 1/4 tone bend on the last note. Play this with your fourth finger but if that's a struggle then use your third finger alongside the fourth to add strength.

There is a lot going on in the exercise so go slow. The main points to consider are the constant motion of your plectrum (subdividing those beats into 1/16ths) and accenting beats 1 and 4. Check out the audio to get a feel for this complex idea.

Example 4e

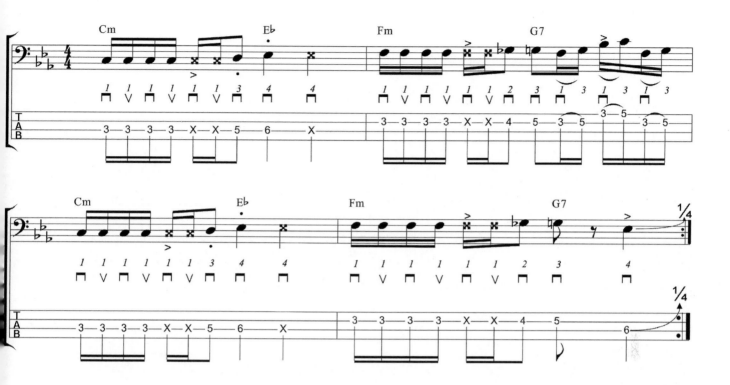

The next idea is a fun one built from three descending ii V patterns using slides and chords. The chord formed is a minor seventh shape rooted on the A string:

Minor 7 Chord Shape (A string root)

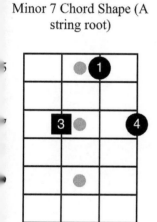

You can slide into the chord with your third finger from anywhere, but try starting from around two or three frets below the target.

39

It's quite tricky to finger all the notes of the chord while allowing them to ring out. To help, curl your fretting hand fingers and play right on the fingertips. Play the first note of the second bar with your first finger so that you then have a nice run up to slide to the next notes.

The final four notes of the bar are the 7th and 10th (3rd) of the F#7 chord. These notes are cool to play separately or together to create a double-stop.

Example 4f

Example 4g is a slap exercise containing swung 1/8th notes and straight 1/16th note triplets to bring ou your inner drummer. This exercise works on the coordination of left and right hands to create fast, complex sounding figures.

Listen to the audio to hear how the swung quavers should be played. A lot of slap playing is down to th interaction of both hands – a bit like how you create rhythms by drumming on a table. The slapping an popping make it look as though the right hand is where the rhythms are coming from. However, it's the frettin hand articulations that create the complex rhythms.

Play through the 1/16th note section slowly, keeping all movements as minimal as possible. The timing betwee the two hands is the key here. Isolate this section and work up to full tempo (around 90 bpm) but only whe you have the articulations down at slow speed.

In bars three and four the pattern is the same except starting on the A string. The only tricky part here is nailing beat 1 on the transition to the different string. As with any slap exercise, pay attention to unwanted noise and cut it out by muting with the fretting hand.

Example 4g

The next chord progression is I ii IV V ii (G major, A minor, C major, D major, A minor) in the key of G Major, and uses some double stops in 3rds and arpeggios voiced Root, 5, 3. Bar three contains a fast 1/16th note run that will get the plucking hand fingers working, as well as get the timing tight between both hands.

Play the double-stops with your first and fourth fingers and pluck with your index and middle fingers. You will have to move quickly to the arpeggio on the 3rd beat, but you do have a 1/4 note rest in which to make the leap. It is important to set your hand in the shape you need as the voicing requires notes to be played in quick succession on the E, D then G strings.

When you play the phrase starting on beat 3 of bar one (over the A minor chord), do not move your first finger after fretting the A on the 5th fret of the E string because there isn't enough time to move the finger to the 5th fret of the G string and then play the next double-stop. Instead, keep your fretting hand in one position and play the C with the bottom part of your first finger. This is awkward to do at first, but you will get it with practice. Practise going from the A to the C using this technique. It's not something us bass players normally do but a useful technique nonetheless.

Use your first finger to roll from the 5th fret notes on the D to G strings and then A to D strings in bar three. You then have a half-beat rest to get back to the start again so shift position quickly.

Example 4h

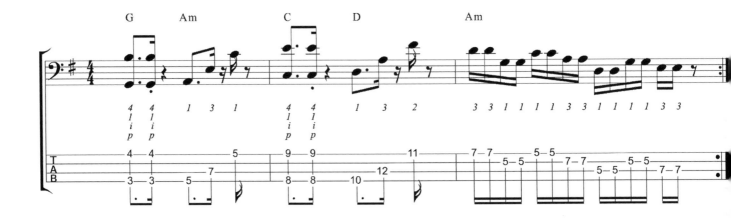

The minor pentatonic scale is one of the most useful scales in any style of music and you should know it inside out on your bass. The next example uses the G Minor pentatonic scale and takes inspiration from Norman Watt Roy's killer bass line on *Hit Me With Your Rhythm Stick* by Ian Dury and the Blockheads.

The First Two Shapes of G Minor Pentatonic

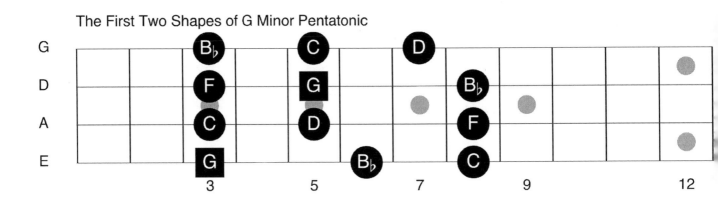

It is hard to play 1/16th notes evenly when they move so quickly across all the strings. Ensure all the notes are the same length and you strictly alternate you picking hand fingers. I find it much easier to pluck the first and second notes of the bar in this example with my index finger. It falls so much easier under the fingers when you play fast, evenly grouped notes like this.

This exercise uses the first two shapes of G Minor pentatonic across all four strings of the bass. For a further workout, and to learn the rest of the pentatonic shapes, move through the remaining shapes in a similar way.

The 5 Shapes of G Minor Pentatonic

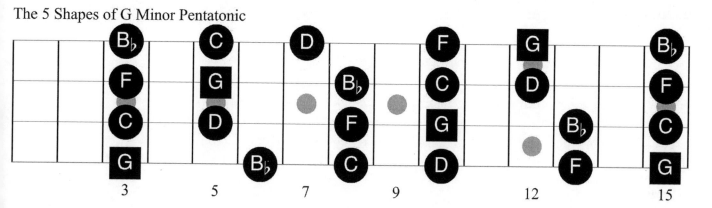

Example 4i

Hammer-ons and pull-offs sounds so good on the bass when they are played with attitude and are bang in time. The next example has a 1/16th note triplet hammer-on/pull-off lick followed by a pull off on the last 1/16th note of beat 3. The main focus of this exercise should be getting this pull-off in time without anticipating the note.

Bar one is just a set up for the action that takes place in bar two. For the hammer-on/pull-off to speak you need to keep your third finger curled and slightly rigid, so that when you hammer on to the 3rd fret, the note is as loud as a fretted note. To get the volume correct for the pull-off, ensure you flick the 3rd finger down towards the floor. Imagine that you are plucking the string with the third finger of your fretting hand. Work on this (as well as hammer-ons) until you achieve a consistent volume between plucked notes, hammer-ons and pull-offs. Then you can start having fun with these articulations, which are the gateway to other techniques such as slapping and tapping.

The timing of the F on the 10th fret of the G string in bar two is awkward to say the least. It is played on the final 1/16th note of the beat and is much harder than playing a note on the beat or half-beat. Isolate this section and count, subdividing the beat so you can hit that note in the correct place.

I make a sound in my head like this: "**da** ga da ga, **da** ga da ga, **da** ga da ga, **da** ga da ga" with the syllable in bold being the beat. You can say this sound fast, which is why I do it. So, the F would be on the second "ga" of beat 3.

The point is that you need some kind of counting system when subdividing beats into 1/16ths otherwise you will be guessing the rhythm and your playing will be inaccurate. You can practise this while walking outside (although you might look a bit weird if you're concentrating too hard!). Make each step a beat and then subdivide each one into four 1/16ths using the *da ga da ga* sound. This will help your timing, groove and sense of rhythm no end! A strong sense of rhythm is the most important tool a bass player can have.

Example 4j

Rock

Like jazz, rock cannot be defined by just one style – there is so much more to the genre. However, some features are undeniably rock, and in this chapter the exercises reflect that. Rock basslines are often solid, "meat and potato" type lines, yet sometimes require more intricate techniques in progressive styles.

A common element of rock bass playing is attitude. Even when playing a relatively simple line, the way you attack the notes (as well as your tone) will dictate whether it sounds rocky or not. One way to get an up-front aggressive sound is to use a pick and use only downstrokes to create a driving feel , which is perfect for this type of line. It can test your stamina to keep this energy going throughout a track, so practising endurance is the key, but do stop if you feel any strain at all.

In Example 5a, concentrate on keeping all the notes at the same intensity without speeding up or slowing down. 1/8th notes are a staple of rock bass playing and deceptively difficult to play really well. In bars three and four, use your fourth finger on the 3rd fret notes instead of your third finger if you find that easier.

Aim to play this exercise up to around 150 bpm, but as always, start slow and speed up gradually.

Example 5a

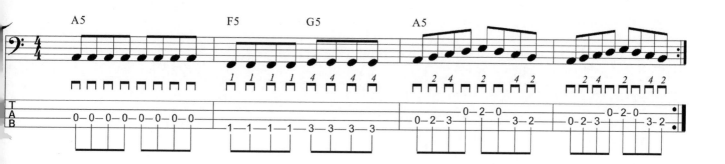

Example 5b is identical but now uses alternate picking. It can be more difficult to keep the notes consistent, as down and up strokes do sound slightly different, so concentrate on keeping everything even. The benefit of alternate picking is increased speed, so the payoff is definitely worth it.

Keep the heel of your picking hand anchored on the E string when you are not playing it, and get some added stability by lightly resting your wrist on the upper bout of the body wherever it is comfortable to do so. This anchoring will keep your body steady and allow the mechanics of your down and up strokes to be machine like. Keep the picking movements tiny to increase your economy of motion and ensure that the pick does not travel too far in either direction after striking the string.

If you cut out waste and inefficiency in your movements you will be well on the road to excellent bass playing.

Example 5b

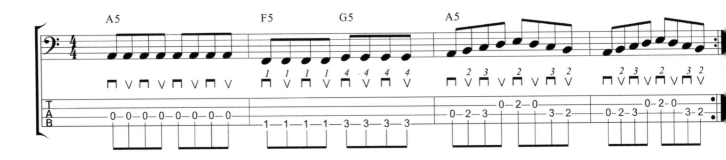

A much-used technique in rock bass playing is to use open strings while playing along the neck. *Hysteria* by Muse is an excellent example of this and the next exercise uses a similar idea. This is a great exercise to open up the fretboard and learn to play in different positions high up on the neck

When playing the open string, you create the split second you need to shift your fretting hand into position, so execute the shift immediately after fretting the previous note.

There are many ways to navigate from the 2nd to the 12th fret, but follow the suggested fingering pattern at first. However, do explore other ways if you find any. As long as the line remains fluid and there are no stumbles it's fine.

Pluck the first note with your index finger then maintain a strict alternate plucking technique. This ensures that the longer middle finger always plays the D string while the index plays the A string and sits comfortably under the fingers. Try starting the exercise plucking with the middle finger and see how uncomfortable that feels!

Example 5c

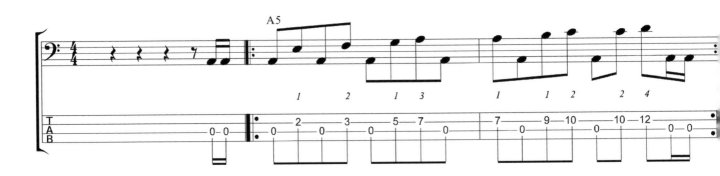

Keeping with the open string theme, this exercise uses the brilliantly named *Phrygian Dominant* mode. This is the fifth mode of the Harmonic Minor scale and the b2 interval coupled with the major 3rd in the first two notes sounds wickedly metal.

The 3/4 time signature presents an interesting plucking hand challenge. Whichever finger you start with, you will always begin the next bar with the other finger. So, if you first pluck with your index finger, the middle finger will land on beat 1 of the next bar and vice versa.

As with the previous example, the fretting hand shifts take place when the open strings are plucked. The two 1/16th notes at the beginning of the bar are quite tricky to play in time, so get those index and middle fingers working overtime. To focus on that rhythm, isolate the first three E notes (two 1/16th notes and one 1/8th note) and cycle round them getting them to pop out.

Example 5d

The next example is based around a iii IV (E minor to F major) chord progression in the key of C Major. This exercise uses the modes formed from each of those chords (E Phrygian and F Lydian) and is reminiscent of a Dream Theater unison line.

The first two bars sit comfortably under the fingers but the transition from bar two to three requires a quick shift with the first finger of the fretting hand. This sets you up to play three notes on the same string across five frets. Pay attention to the fingering pattern here. On the repeat, quickly shift your first finger back to the 7th fret of the A string (E).

The trickiest part of this exercise is to articulate the 1/8th note and two 1/16th notes rhythm and it will test your pizzicato skills.

Example 5e

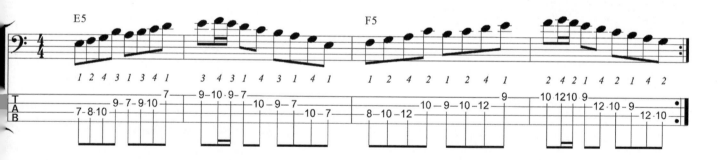

I am a huge fan of progressive rock and this next exercise pays homage to Steve Vai, who loves to use all kinds of complex harmonies and meters. This exercise might hurt your brain for a bit, since the time signature shifts from 11/16 to 12/16. Stick with it though, as it's much easier than you think.

The key to cracking odd time signatures (odd by name and by nature!) is to split them up into manageable chunks. This example was written around comfortable and achievable left and right-hand patterns using slaps, pops and hammer-ons. Once you figure it out, you will see that it flows under the fingers fairly easily.

11/16 means that there are eleven 1/16th notes in a bar. Unfortunately, there's no real way to describe how to count this on paper without it sounding complicated, but I'll give it a go!

The first trick is to *not* count eleven 1/16th notes in your head – instead, split it up. Tap your foot in eight notes and keep the 1/16th notes going steadily in your head, so that each foot tap contains two 1/16th notes. As the first four notes of this example are all 1/8th notes you can count "one, two, three, four" simply by following your foot.

The next tap is the tricky moment. This tap lasts for three 1/16ths, so after you count "one, two, three, four", count "one, two, three" in 1/16ths (double the speed of the eights you were tapping). Go slow until you get it and follow the slap, pop and hammer-on markings closely until the notes feel comfortable under the fingers. Listen to the audio and try to count along for a while before playing.

Split up bar four as well. This bar is in 12/16 and you can see from the groupings of 1/16th notes that there is a group of seven followed by a five (making twelve 1/16ths in the bar). You can see why people say its music meets maths!

Play the pops with your index finger until you hit bar four where you use your middle finger as indicated. The index finger doesn't have time to get to the G string after plucking the F. Return to the index for the next pop. Play the group of seven slowly, then the group of five. When you're confident, combine the whole bar.

If you're not used to playing in odd time signatures this will take some getting used to, but it's so satisfying when you get it down!

Example 5f

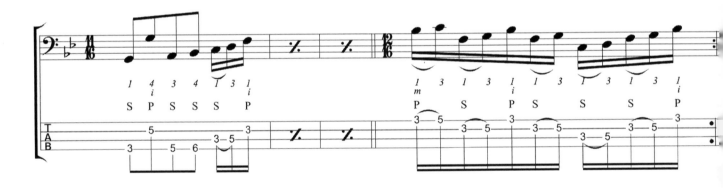

Les Claypool of Primus is clearly influenced by the jazz great Stanley Clarke, especially his use of strums and slap. This next exercise uses a Primus style line with a touch of Flea to get a rock slap vibe. The "5" next to each chord denotes a *power chord* which is simply a chord containing the Root and 5th. A power chord played with distortion is the secret to a lot of rock rhythm guitar playing. They also sound incredibly full and powerful on bass.

You can play these chords with the nail of your strumming hand index finger as if you were holding a pick or use a *brush stroke* which is denoted by the arrow in the TAB and strummed with the fleshy part of your thumb. Use down strokes and experiment with both brush strokes and strums.

The double-stop on beat 2 is played by barring your first finger so you won't miss a beat when you pop the two notes with your index and middle fingers.

To integrate the slap with the strums, the important thing is to stay compact with your movements. It's tempting to give the strums a Pete Townsend style windmill, but then you will be nowhere near the 5th fret for the next pop so make the strum a small movement.

Notice how a lot of techniques require small movements to achieve real precision.

Example 5g

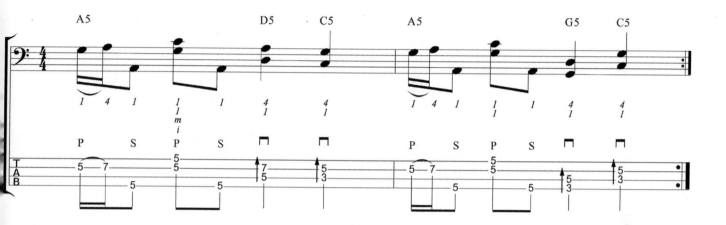

There are a variety of different string bending techniques and this next exercise works on three of them. These are the standard string bend, pre-bend/release, and bend/release. They all have slightly different flavours and require different touches. Where you see "1/2" written in the TAB it denotes a semitone bend.

Use the second finger to support the third finger whenever you attempt any bend in this exercise. This gives you much more control and will enable you bend more in tune. You will need the strength from both fingers in bar two to play the full-tone bend. Try playing the destination pitch before attempting the bend as this will train your ears and fingers to accurately hit the destination pitch.

The bend in bar three is a prebend/release. After the first three plucked notes you have a gap of two 1/8th notes to bend the 5th fret of the G string up a semitone *without* plucking. This is the pre-bend. Once plucked, simply release the note back to pitch (C).

The bend/release in the final bar is similar, except that you do pluck the first note as you bend. Once you have bent the note up a semitone, release it back to the C so that you hear the pitch changing. Listen to the audio to hear these subtle differences.

Example 5h

Billy Sheehan is arguably the king of explosive rock bass technique and this next exercise is a nod to him. The line uses the *legato* (smooth melodies created with hammer-ons and pull-offs) technique to create a smoother sound than plucked notes. In this example, hammer-ons are patterns from the A Natural Minor scale.

In beat 3 of the first bar, your fretting hand should be in sixth position. To play the G on the 5th fret of the D string, your first finger must stretch out of this position. This is sometimes called extended fingering and is useful when playing complex patterns on the bass. It's a bit of a stretch, but a common hand shape nonetheless.

Keep the fingers relaxed and curled as you hammer onto the notes. The final note of each phrase should be played staccato to help you practise your fretting hand touch and you will have to be dextrous to follow the hammer-ons with such a short note.

The fourth finger is used a lot in this exercise and this will help you build its strength. A common hurdle in developing bass technique is having a weak fourth finger and relying too much on the first, second and third. Good bass players' fourth fingers are always as strong as their others.

Example 5i

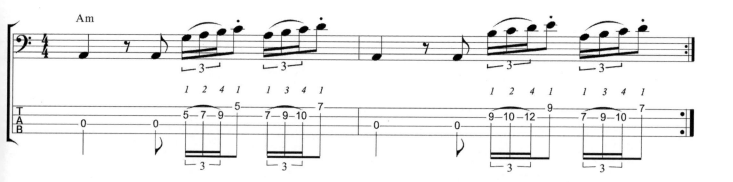

Example 5j uses *two handed tapping* to create a challenging line that contains 1/16th notes and 1/16th note triplets. There is no need to play this exercise too quickly but it does sound great around 110 bpm. The little crosses above every note denote a tap by a left- or right-hand finger. These taps are brilliant for working on finger strength.

The fingering is notated under every note and it is important to stick to what's written. This looks a bit scarier on paper than it actually is, but you may still have to learn each beat in turn and piece it together.

All the notes come from this familiar B Minor Pentatonic shape.

B Minor Pentatonic

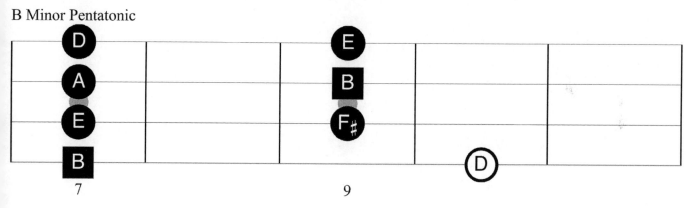

With a bit of practice, you will find that this line fits comfortably under the fingers. It helps to know your fretboard well enough that you can apply advanced techniques to simple patterns to create some unusual lines. They often sound impressive and "difficult" while actually being relatively easy once you have the core technique down.

Playing the accents notated gives the exercise an extra rhythmical dimension that will develop your coordination and touch. Add these accents in when you can play the notes confidently.

Example 5j

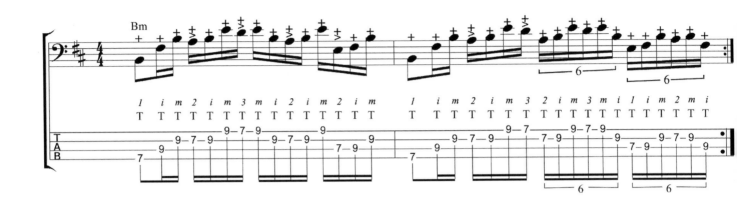

Jazz

The humble bass player can easily be intimidated by jazz with its extended chord symbols, modes, substitutions, complex harmonies and technical requirements. However, much beauty lies within, from the familiar roots of blues, to the infectious rhythms of Brazilian and African music, and the harmonic innovations of the bebop era onwards. Whether or not you like jazz there is much to gain from studying it. It's a bit like eating vegetables: even if you don't like them, you have to admit they're good for you!

The exercises in this chapter focus on some aspects of jazz that will help improve your ear, technique and knowledge of music theory.

~

Playing a walking bassline or a solo over a ii V I chord progression is central to jazz. Jazz tunes often *modulate* (change key) which makes keeping up trickier than a rock or pop tune that often stays in the same key throughout. This makes knowing which scales and arpeggios fit each chord essential.

A bass player will always play scale notes, arpeggio notes, or some combination of the two. Over the ii chord you play the Dorian mode, over the V chord the Mixolydian mode, and over the I chord the Ionian mode (this is another name for the major scale you already know).

Example 6a is a descending ii V I exercise using arpeggios. It starts in the key of D Major then moves down a tone (two frets) to C Major. Watch out for the first finger stretch in the first bar over the minor seventh arpeggio.

When you get to the end of the notated exercise, carry on until you run out of fretboard. Ensure you are 100% aware of what arpeggio you are playing, the function of it (whether it is the ii, the V or the I) and what interval you are playing – Root, 3rd, 5th or 7th. Altering the order of notes you play, as well as the rhythm, will make the line sound more like a walking bass line or solo. Try it!

Example 6a

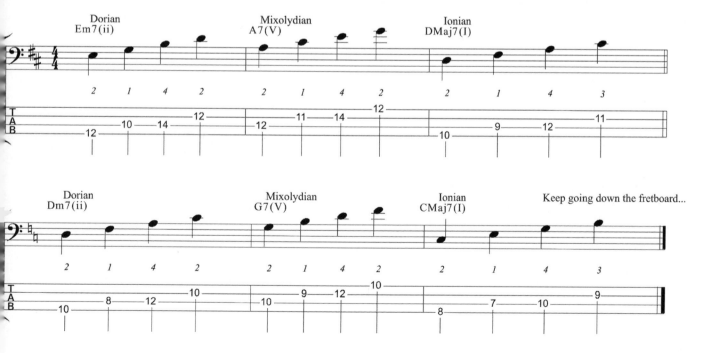

Let's now play through the same progression, but this time ascending and descending through the modes. The arpeggios you played in Example 6a were formed by playing the 1st, 3rd, 5th and 7th notes of each mode in this example and so are completely related. If you always know the mode and the arpeggio formed on each chord, then you'll be good to go when it comes to improvising and constructing basslines.

As you play through this exercise look and listen out for the patterns used. Mapping a pattern to a sound is the best way to train your ear. Again, watch for that first finger stretch over the Dorian mode in the first bar. If you find a different fingering pattern that works, go for it.

Swing is predominant in jazz. This is where each beat is subdivided into triplets, the first two of which are tied together to create *swing 1/8ths*. This is a different ball game to the straight 1/8ths found in many styles of pop and rock. Pay close attention to this feel as it is one of the keys to great jazz bass playing. Listen to the backing track to hear how they should be played.

Example 6b

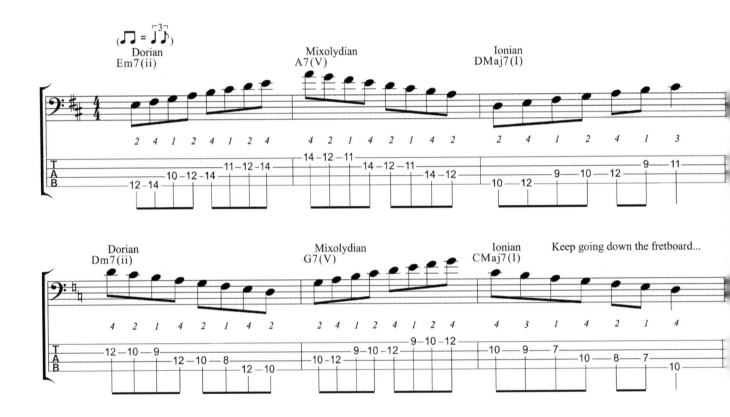

The next example is a jazzy-pop chordal line ascending through the first four chords of Bb Major (Bbmaj7, Cm7, Dm7, Ebmaj7).

Make sure to swing those 1/8ths again and listen to the audio to match my feel. The root note is played with your plucking hand thumb and the top two notes are played with your index and middle fingers. Anchor your wrist on the upper bout of the body to gain stability and keep your digits always hovering right by the strings.

When you feel comfortable, separate out the voices of the chords, and experiment with different rhythms and patterns by playing the chord notes in different orders.

A great exercise is to set the metronome to 60 bpm and feel each click as beats two and four, replicating the backbeat of the drums. When you hear the metronome click, count beat two before counting "three, four" and syncing the four to the next metronome click. Count "one" in the gap and keep going.

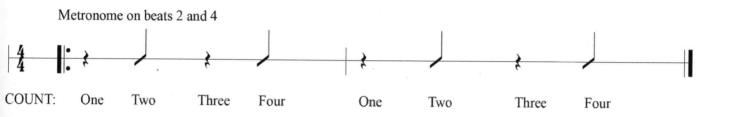

Example 6c

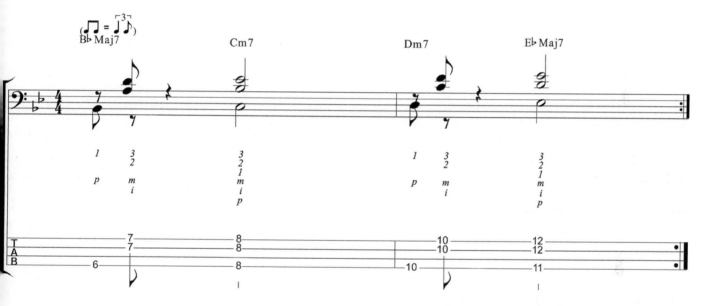

You can play the next example using straight 1/8th notes. It is a solo type line navigating through a I ii iii IV V I (Abmaj7, Bbm7, Cm7, Dbmaj7, Abmaj7) chord progression using arpeggios in the key of Ab Major.

The cool thing about this exercise is that all the notes are played in a single position. This type of line could be used in a solo, but if you know the notes of the arpeggio you are playing then it is equally as good when playing strong walking lines. Ensure you map out and memorise the arpeggios found in this position and then transpose them to other keys.

Example 6d

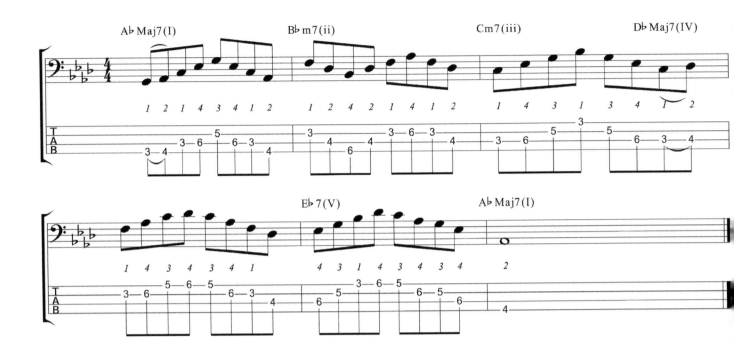

As a youngster, I remember being extremely confused by jazz. "Why can't we just stick to Root and 5th like in rock and pop?" I soon learned to love and appreciate it, but it was terms like *extensions* that got me confused!

Extensions occur when you play notes beyond the 7th in an arpeggio. An arpeggio is formed by starting on the first note of a scale then playing every other note in 3rds. This forms the 1st, 3rd, 5th, 7th, 9th, 11th and 13th intervals. Notice that there are seven notes in total which is the same number of notes as in the scale. It is essentially like playing the notes of a scale stacked in 3rds (played vertically) rather than played stepwise (horizontally). This is an important concept in jazz.

Example 6d takes you through the extensions found in the Dorian mode. You can use these in your solo lines and also when playing walking bass. Pay attention to the TAB and the fingering patterns as the exercise plays the notes of the arpeggio going along the fretboard. Take your time with this and ensure that you know exactly which interval you are playing at all times.

Don't forget to swing the 1/8th notes and I recommend practising with the metronome clicking on beats two and four again, as in Example 6b.

Example 6e

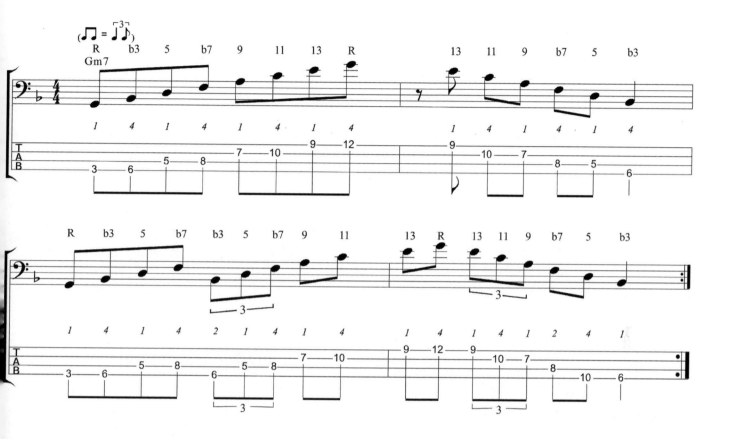

The coolest thing about jazz is how many musical genres are incorporated – everything from rock to blues to old school RnB. If you listen to bands like Weather Report, you'll hear a lot of musical exploration going on. This exercise is influenced by Jaco Pastorius' use of RnB and funk in his playing and includes ghost notes and raking.

Example 6e is in the key of C Major and uses a I iii ii (C major, E minor, D minor) chord progression. Notice how the two minor chords in bars three and four use an identical pattern. You can apply these patterns to any style you like.

The key to this exercise is the raking of your index finger from the D to the E strings, so isolate these three notes and get used to the timing, especially of the ghost note. The first note in each group of three notes is fretted with your fourth finger. To play the ghost note use a combination of the remaining fingers which should be laying across the strings at this point.

Set your metronome at around 90 bpm and focus on making all the notes pop out with energy and good feel. Listen to the song *Black Market* from the 1979 Weather Report album *8:30* to get an idea of what I mean.

Example 6f

Now for a challenging fingerstyle Bossa Nova-style exercise with a slight touch of the Mario Brothers theme about it.

Example 6g is a I ii V (Amaj7, Bm7, E7) chord sequence in A Major that uses the index and middle fingers to pluck two notes of the chord while playing a simple Root and 5th bassline with the thumb. This is great for building independence, time keeping and fingerstyle technique.

All the bassline notes plucked with the thumb land on the beat, so there's nothing difficult there. It is the higher notes plucked with the index and middle fingers that might pose a problem if you've never used this technique before. Listen to the audio example, but also study the notation. The rhythmic figure remains constant throughout, so once you've cracked it, just concentrate on moving from one chord shape to the next as quickly as you can. Listen to the audio if you are unsure of the rhythm.

Practise the shift between chords slowly. Moving more than one finger to a fret at the same time is not a skill most bass players use, so you may find it tricky at first. Keep going though, and build up the speed gradually.

Here is an optional add-on to this example. Only attempt this once you have the exercise completely down. Play through the same exercise while tapping your foot along to a *clave* rather than all the beats as you should be used to. A clave is a repetitive rhythmic pattern used in Latin music. There is a 3:2 clave and a 2:3 clave. Try both. Listen to the audio examples where you will hear each clave followed by the example.

WARNING: this may be one of the most difficult things to do in the whole book! It's a great way of building independence and develops your groove while achieving something downright difficult.

The way to crack this is to slow everything down and split the line up into tiny chunks. For example, when you tap the 2:3 clave, you will realise that you always start plucking an 1/8th note before you tap the first two hits of the clave. Then you realise that the first of the next three hits land on beat 3 when your thumb plays the A. Keep piecing it together in this manner like a jigsaw puzzle, repeating bigger and bigger sections until it comes together.

This exercise is a good one to get you practising how to practice. You will have to be patient, break the exercise down, repeat it, piece it together and go through the frustration of not being able to do it before coming out the other side. This is one of the most important lessons to learn from this book and you will have a real sense of achievement when you master this discipline. Take your time and keep it as a goal to work to.

Example 6g

Jazz is such a rich art form and the musical creativity stemming from the genre is endless. One of the reasons for this is the harmony that comes from the use of modes and different minor scales. Something not so common in styles such as pop and rock is the use of the Melodic Minor scale and its modes.

Example 6h uses one of the most useful of these modes – the Super Locrian (also called the Altered Scale or Diminished Whole Tone scale). The reason I like the last name best is that this mode starts off as a diminished scale (going up a semitone then a tone then another semitone) then becomes a whole tone scale (which goes up in tones). This name describes how to play the scale and removes the complexity that the name Super Locrian implies. In any case, it is an awesome scale to use over altered dominant chords.

This line ascends and descends the mode using some hammer-ons and pull-offs to emulate a sax player's phrasing. Play it as fluidly and smoothly as you can and tune your ear into the unusual intervals that this scale creates. Also, look out for the scale patterns mentioned in the previous paragraph. If you are only used to major and minor scales then this will feel, sound and look unfamiliar, but with some repetition, you can incorporate it into your playing.

Example 6h

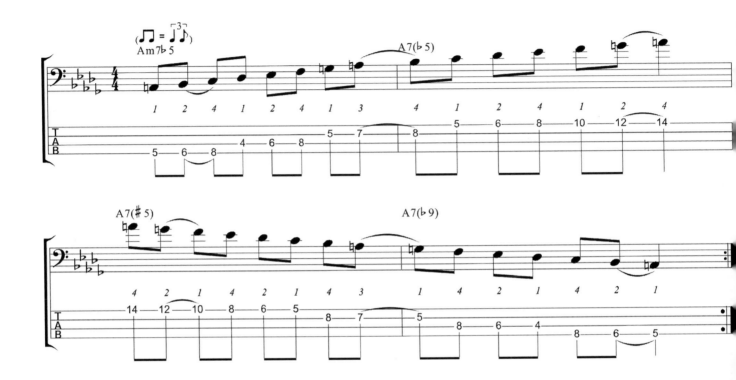

Example 6i harmonises the G Melodic Minor scale in seventh arpeggios in a Latin style. This harmony is important to absorb if you want to get into jazz. There are many interesting features of the harmonised Melodic Minor scale including a minor/major and an augmented chord.

The construction of a Melodic Minor scale is:

Tone, semitone, tone, tone, tone, tone, semitone.

Keep this in mind as you navigate this exercise and explore the scale. It's easy to remember the two consecutive dominant seventh arpeggios (C7, D7) and minor seven flat five arpeggios (Em7b5, F#m7b5) you build from the fourth to the seventh notes of the scale. Loads of amazing jazz tunes come from this harmony so I recommend you learn this exercise inside out.

Example 6i

The final example in this chapter uses a V IV (E7 to D7) progression in A Melodic Minor. There are some legato slides and dominant seventh chords, and it sounds a bit like *Elephant Talk* by King Crimson. It is typical of the kind of angular sound you can get from the Melodic Minor.

The three notes that make up the legato slide are played by plucking the first (D on the 7th fret) and then sliding to the second note (E on the 9th fret) then back again. The challenge is keeping the line steady while performing a mixture of plucking and sliding. There is an 1/8th note rest at the end of the bar to give you just enough time to get to the 10th fret for the D7 chord, but you must be quick!

As you move to fret the notes of the chord, shift your first, second and fourth fingers so that they are pre-prepared to play the notes. Use your thumb, index and middle fingers to pluck the chords and use the fret markers to help you hit the exact spot by looking where you need to end up just before you get there.

Example 6j

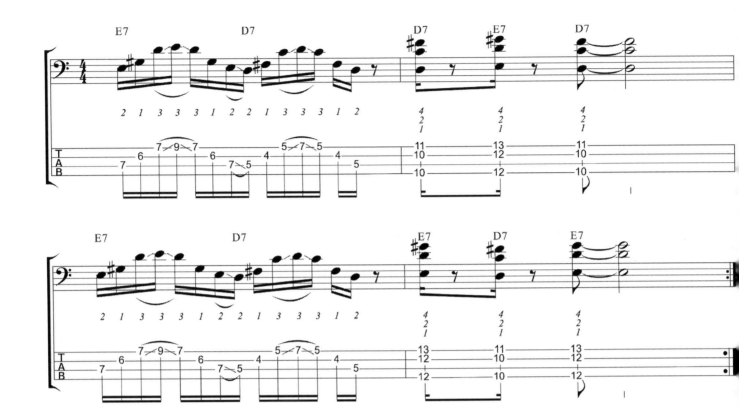

Drone Exercises

A drone is a constant single note that rings out over a period of time. Playing scales over drones gives you the opportunity to hear the sound of the intervals working together and gives you a brilliant reference point to investigate the moods that the scales create. In short, it's an amazing practice for strengthening your ear – an extremely important goal for any musician.

The exercises in this chapter work on various techniques while using the seven modes of the major scale (Ionian, Dorian, Phrygian, Lydian, Mixolydian, Aeolian and Locrian). The important points to note are the sounds, colours and moods that the different modes create. This is an excellent way to get your head around why modes are important, what they are, and how to use them – all while building your technique.

Memorise the patterns and see if you can transpose the lines to the other 12 keys.

Example 7a starts with the G Ionian mode (major scale), so use the G drone backing track for this exercise. The exercise moves through the notes of the mode playing a Root, 6th and 3rd (10th) each time, before sliding into the next pattern.

Shape of My Heart by Sting uses a similar type of pattern on guitar.

Use some of these shapes as a springboard to a composition. Play the patterns in different orders and rhythms to make up cool basslines and interesting chord voicings. I recommend learning some basic piano or guitar to play simple chord progressions to help develop your writing and production skills.

Pluck the first note and slide into the next where indicated (don't pluck the note you slide into).

Example 7a

Example 7b slides back down through the same patterns. Once you have this example down, combine it with Example 7a.

Example 7b

For the next example you have to imagine that your bass only has a G and D string. Playing on just two strings is a brilliant way to create unusual phrases, fills and lines and to get you out of the same old patterns we all fall into. This exercise explores that idea using an E Dorian mode, so use the E drone backing track.

Don't be put off by the appearance of the lesser-spotted 1/32nd notes here! There are eight them in one beat but setting your metronome to 60 bpm slows you right down, and you can build up speed from there.

This idea contains an interesting syncopation created by grouping the first thirteen 1/16th notes in a seven then a six. This sounds cool with the notated accents so try and emphasise those. Listen closely to the audio example to hear this in action.

The fast bits in each bar are played by immediately pulling off your third finger after the hammer-on. Be committed to the shifts when moving as you have to be quick to play the first note of the bar on the beat.

Example 7c

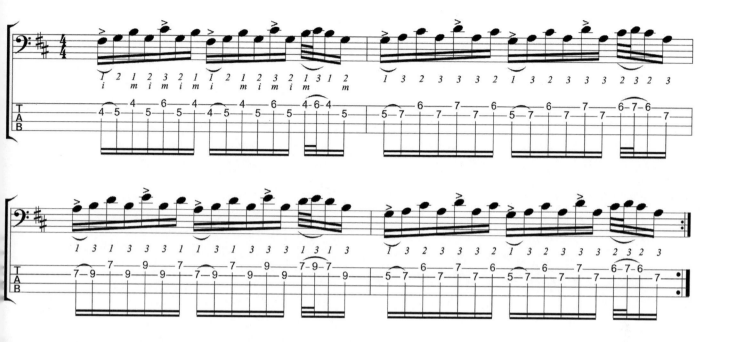

Moving onto the third mode, Phrygian, Example 7d is an alternate fingering and one-finger-per-fret work-out. Aim to play this accurately up to around 160 bpm, but start slower if you need to. This exercise plays through the mode in thirds, missing a note each time then returning to it. The fretting hand stays in one position but you constantly jump to different strings, so your hands will need to be coordinated to build any kind of speed.

Note the dark sound created by the minor 2nd between the first and second notes. This mode is sometimes called the Spanish scale and you can hear why when you play this to the C drone backing track.

Example 7d

Here's a great test for your fretting hand's third and fourth fingers. Use the E drone for this exercise in E Lydian. The time signature is 7/16 which is made by splitting the bar up into two groups of two 1/16th notes followed by a three.

Play hammer-ons ascending and pull-offs on the way back down. It is when descending that the third and fourth fingers are really challenged and it will feel quite horrible! Use this to strengthen and speed up these weaker fingers.

Keep the right-hand fingers alternating as indicated. Again, this is especially difficult when descending as there is a temptation to rake one finger down the strings. It's much more difficult to alternate when string crossing down the strings in the direction of G to E. You may need to slow bars three and four right down until you get used to it.

Example 7e

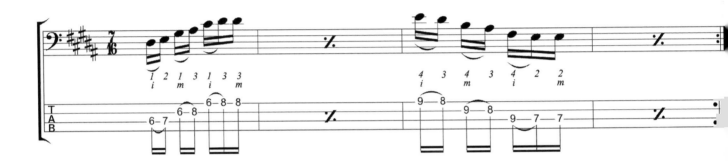

Vibrato is one of the most expressive techniques musicians use and sounds beautiful on bass. There are a couple of ways to play vibrato. One is to fret the note and perform a series of mini-bends – moving the string up and down in the direction of floor to ceiling. You can change the speed to alter exactly how your vibrato rings out. The other way is to keep your finger pressed into the fretboard and to wiggle your finger across the plane of the string (in the direction of the body of the bass to the headstock). This is subtler and a bit trickier to do.

Vibrato is personal to every player and will contribute to your unique voice on the instrument. Make it sound as musical as you can and avoid too much speed and wiggling of the string (unless that's the sound you are going for!). Vibrato is a great tool when soloing, but an acquired taste and possibly best avoided when playing regular basslines.

Use just one fretting hand finger throughout each run through the exercise, but have a go using all fingers. The only other thing to watch for in this example is the slides. Aim to land exactly on the note without over or under shooting the mark.

Experiment with the speed of the vibrato as well as the type you use. Don't bother with a metronome for this exercise as the goal is to sit with the vibrato and listen. Use the E drone again as this exercise is in Mixolydian.

Example 7f

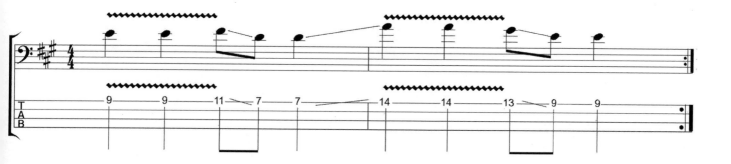

Example 7g combines many of the tricks and techniques you've used in the book already, such as taps, hammer-ons, pull-offs and quick hand shifts. The exercise develops your two-handed tapping and is excellent for building strength, speed and stamina. It is written in A Aeolian, so use the A drone backing track.

In this exercise, use the index finger of your tapping hand to play the indicated notes. At the same time, rest your thumb on the E or A string to provide an anchor, so that the tapping index finger can remain steady and consistent throughout.

In the first bar, tap the 14th fret with your index finger while holding the 9th fret down with your first finger. Immediately after tapping the 14th fret, flick the string downward so you come to rest on the D string. This will pull the note on the 14th fret off to the 9th fret. Next, hammer the second finger of your fretting hand down onto the 10th fret. Start learning this example by trying to get just those three notes flowing smoothly.

The next three notes are similar. Place both your first finger on the 9th fret *and* your second finger on the 10th fret. After you tap with your fretting index finger, pull off to the 10th fret. Then pull off from the 10th to the 9th fret making sure to flick the string downwards.

When you slowly piece all this together you will see how elegantly the notes fit together under your fingers. Listen to the audio example to hear how it should go and, as ever, start without a metronome until you feel comfortable with the mechanics, then add the click. Start slowly and aim for 120 bpm.

This exercise calls for excellent technique and it's tough to make it flow in time. Remember that in order to play fast, you first have to play slow. Master it perfectly at a slow, manageable speed before building it up. This will ensure the technique supports the execution of the line.

Example 7g

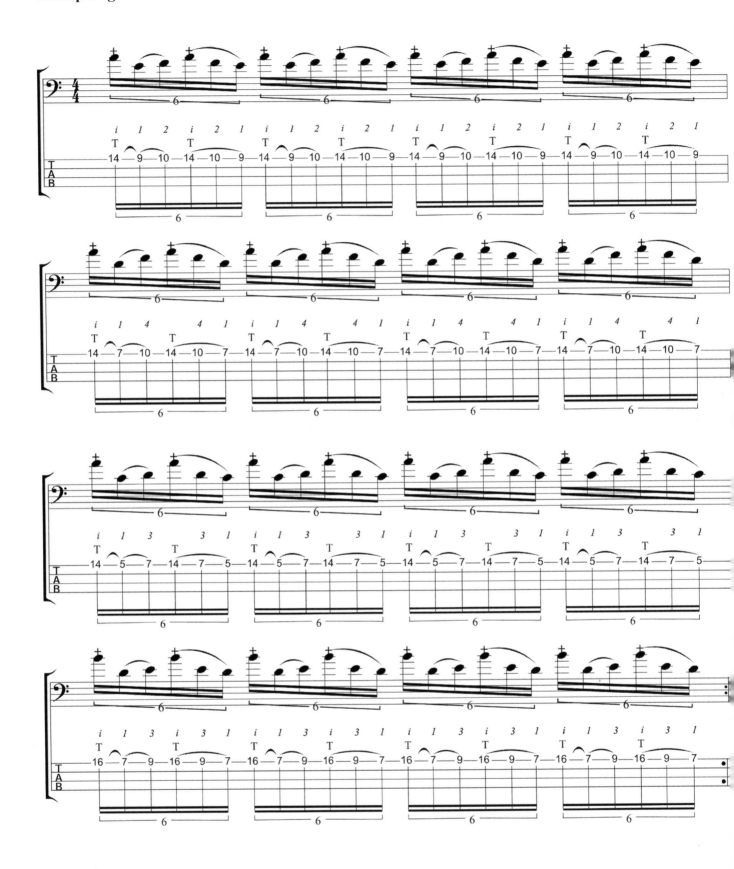

The next exercise is A Locrian, so use the A drone note backing track. It is written in 3/4, uses 1/8th note and is especially good for developing the third and fourth fingers of your fretting hand as well as helping yo practise your string crossing technique. Use strict alternate fingering (or picking) and follow the fretting hand fingerings. Begin with a down stroke and alternate from there. Regardless of whether you use pick or fingers, take care to mute the strings to avoid unwanted noise when ascending, by placing your plucking hand thumb on the E or A strings when you're not playing them.

Recording yourself and listening back with a critical (but calm) ear is a great way to find out what needs attention.

Example 7h

The diminished scale is an eight-note symmetrical scale (meaning it is formed from the same repeated interval pattern). I would describe the sound created as strangely beautiful. This exercise works over an E drone or you could just pluck your open E string as you play the notes. As you play through the exercise notice how the interval pattern repeats every three frets.

The double-stops in the last two bars are a great dexterity exercise for the fretting hand. Use your index and middle fingers to pluck these notes. I'm sure there's a piece of music in the score of the original Predator movie that uses a similar idea to the repeated diminished double-stops. It's dissonant and unsettling, which I guess you want when there's a monster stalking you. Learning different modes and scales broadens your sonic palette and makes you a more creative musician.

Once you have the symmetrical pattern under your fingers you can come up with all kinds of lines across the fretboard using all the strings. Mix up rhythms and techniques to create more phrases.

Example 7i

When you are confronted with a new scale it's a great idea to use a drone note in your practice to get the flavour of it.

Example 7j uses the Mixolydian b6 mode (also known as the Hindu scale) which is a beautiful sound and a mode of the Melodic Minor scale. The line in this example could easily be used in a song by bands like Led Zeppelin, who were big fans of the Melodic Minor scale as well as other exotic sounding modes. Use the E drone for this exercise then learn the pattern in other keys.

The legato slide in the first bar is played with the fourth finger. It's quite a big slide and requires strength in the finger, so take that part slowly. Pay attention to the slightly unusual fingering choices; they do work and get the fingers in position without having to shift around too much.

Example 7j

Next Steps

I hope the exercises in this book have challenged you and inspired you to think about bass playing not just from a technical standpoint, but with theory, feel, groove, timing, phrasing and your ears in mind too. Being as good as you possibly can means continuously making small improvements in these key areas of musicianship and I hope you will continue to do so as you continue your musical journey.

Remember that you can become as good as you want to be if you have clearly defined goals and a consistent practice routine. If you master the fundamentals on bass, your bandmates will love you.

I'd be absolutely delighted if you joined me at my website **www.onlinebasscourses.com** where I produce lessons, blog posts, tips and courses on all things bass. If you have any questions, I'd also love to hear from you.

You can contact me through the site where you will also find all my social media details.

More Great Bass Books from Fundamental Changes

Electric Bass Improve Your Groove

- Discover how to groove flawlessly on electric bass in any style of music
- Understand bass guitar rhythm and placement
- Play in the pocket, every time.

The Bass Technique Finger Gym

- Proven technical exercises to supercharge your progress
- Turn technique into licks with essential lick-building exercises
- Learn to build speed, slap and pop

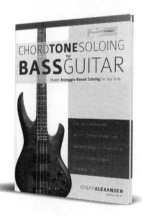

Chord Tone Soloing for Bass Guitar

- Master Jazz Arpeggios and use them like a pro in your solos
- Learn how to solo over 13 Essential Progressions
- Spice up your bass skills with Extensions and Substitutions

Sight Reading Mastery for Bass Guitar

- Pitch Recognition
- Instant Location of Notes
- Unlimited Exercises
- All Keys

Printed in Great Britain
by Amazon

12904608R00043